This book is to be returned on or before
the last date stamped below.

NORTH BIRMINGHAM
SCHOOL OF NURSING

EDUCATION for HEALTH

A guide for health visitors, nurses
and all others working in the community

Marion S Strehlow, BA, SRN, HV, HVT, AMIHE
Education Officer (Health Visiting)
English National Board
formerly Professional Adviser
Council for the Education and Training
of Health Visitors

Harper & Row, Publishers
London

Cambridge
Hagerstown
Philadelphia
New York

San Francisco
Mexico City
Sao Paulo
Sydney

Copyright © 1983 Marion S Strehlow
All rights reserved

Harper & Row Ltd
28 Tavistock Street
London WC2E 7PN

British Library Cataloguing in Publication Data

Strehlow, Marion
   Education for health.
   1. Health education
   I. Title
   613'.07   RA440

   ISBN 0-06-318247-5

Typeset by *Sunrise Setting*, Torquay, Devon
Printed in Great Britain by
Butler & Tanner Ltd, Frome and London

CONTENTS

ACKNOWLEDGEMENTS

Thanks to all those who encouraged me to put pen to paper, especially Beryl Reynolds, Joyce Jameson and Jane Randell. Many thanks, too, to a patient husband who put up with a clacking typewriter during the night and a disorganized household while the process of writing was going on.

CHAPTER 1

INTRODUCTION

Health , which is a state of complete physical, mental and social well-being and not merely the absence of disease or infirmity, is a fundamental human right ...

from WHO (1978) Report on Primary Health Care Conference, Alma Ata 1978 Health for all by the year 2000

Health education has been discussed in most professional journals, it forms part of the staple of newspapers and magazines, part of the qualifying curriculum for most members of caring professions and a large part of the studies and practice of health visitors and school nurses. However, one gains the distinct impression that texts relating to health education are either dull and boring or too technical to be interpreted for reasonable practical use, resulting in confusion and disenchantment. This book does not set out to be a learned treatise, but attempts to combine a very practical approach with some ideas about policies, pressures and presumptions. It also attempts to incorporate a sometimes tongue-in-cheek sense of humour.

Health — the achievement thereof — should be FUN, and should lead to a greater facility to enjoy life in whichever form enjoyment takes for an individual, family or community. Being able to participate actively, think clearly, or make the decision to relax and not think at all, are elements of a healthy life-style. Having the capacity to achieve health and enjoy life as fully as possible makes the processes of decisionmaking on any level easier, and in turn enables a healthier approach to any problem which may be encountered. So why should health education be a formidable task, and rarely regarded as an enjoyable activity?

This book sets out to show that health education can, and should, be onerous and honourable tasks, but that it should also become an enjoyable part of professional practice and, for practitioners and recipients, an

1

enjoyable part of daily living. This volume has been written on the assumption that those interested in reading and using it will already possess basic professional skills, and that many will have progressed far beyond basic practice. The latter may be seeking to consider their present standpoint in a new light, or review what they are doing. Whilst some readers may wish to read from cover to cover, I suggest that a scan, and gradually a study of chapters and references, may be the most useful procedure.

A perspective

Historically speaking, health education has been practised since man first populated the world. One can imagine early man giving his family instructions on how to clean their habitations, explaining that the reason is to avoid attracting the attention of wild animals or vermin, and to make the cave a cosy nest. Early woman would insist that to wash, except under a cold running stream, could cause the most terrifying illnesses, and that to cleanse oneself or one's clothes too frequently might lead to horrendous consequences.

Man's survival depended on physical fitness. Mental aberrations were usually regarded as providing the entertainment of the day, or as inspired by the gods. Some physical differences could be tolerated, but acute handicap brought danger to the whole tribe, and, if allowed to survive, disgrace to parents and the extended family.

In modern society there are remnants of old traditions, which not only follow religious practice, but are also a direct consequence of the rules of health laid down by ancestors whose names and achievements are long forgotten. Examples of this are: the Eskimo custom of leaving the old and ailing on the ice, either to be taken to their gods or as an equivalent of recycling valuable resources; the rule among a large proportion of the nomad populations that the right hand must be used for 'clean' objects, such as foods only, whereas the left hand is reserved for all other tasks; and not least the health rules inherent in superstitious practices.

The development of the siesta or its equivalent bears a direct relationship to the harm which can be caused in tropical countries by excess exposure to sunlight.

Documentation of health rules, as differentiated from salves or cures, can be found within the earliest writings. During the Pharaohs' time the washing of hands before meals was laid down as etiquette and the old Greeks ensured the isolation of infected persons as a preventive measure. It was this practice of isolation which led, most probably, to the development of medicine as a profession — no one wanted to be isolated and, therefore, they sought cures. The Romans made cleanliness into a cult, and we have the evidence of baths galore. The thought that most important economic, political and domestic decisions were made in Roman baths leads one to wonder about the function of modern committee rooms!

It would seem that during the Middle Ages, especially in Europe, health rules, or the fundamentals of good health and hygiene, were kept in abeyance. Washing facilities became fewer, clothes became more cumbersome and less easy to replace and there were the first effects of living in large communities — disease and ill-health. The Italian, Salerno, attempted to arouse interest in health education by publishing a set of rules for health which still ring true today, but were unacceptable to his contemporaries, especially those convinced of the importance of medicinal 'cures'. Of the 15 or 16 rules, one of the most interesting says that shop assistants should not be allowed to scratch their heads or 'private parts' of their bodies whilst handling foods!

Throughout the ages there were fanatics who took health to its extreme. They should stand as guides of what to avoid for the health educator of the 1980s. The Spartans developed a cult of physical fitness, but were overtaken by invaders shortly after they disregarded mental agility. The Olympic games were started as a tribute to extremes of prowess and fitness, and have become a spectacle of international competition. Generally fatness was held to ridicule, except in the Orient where it was acceptable in the very old or very holy.

Documents which originated in ancient times and which are still in use today also contain rules of health. These rules are also the cornerstones of some religious practices and therefore remain vitally important to some groups of people. Because of their current usage they are of note to health educators. The most commonly used rule books are the Old Testament of the Bible, the Koran and their Eastern equivalents. The rules concern themselves with behaviour, such as cleanliness of body and spirit, food practices and guidance for personal relationships.

The content of this book

The approach to health education in this book is essentially practical, based on knowledge gained throughout professional life, an overwhelming interest in the promotion of health and reasonably wide experience as a health worker, in a variety of geographical areas and fields of work, as a teacher and as a consumer of health services. Some statements may appear pragmatic, but they are intended to act as guides for consideration and discussion. It is acknowledged that pragmatism does relate happily with health education, and that flexibility is the essence of practice.

There are five main threads running through the book, although they are interlinked in most chapters. The threads are:

1. *The consumer of health education* is acknowledged as an important contributor to the sum total of efforts and effects. It is not stated, but is implied, that if it were not possible to arouse interest in consumers or clients, then health education would cease as an overt and professional activity. Sales techniques are recommended as a means of arousing initial interest, acknowledging that consumers in general do not consider health education a necessary element of their daily lives, though interest in healthy practices is increasing rapidly. Full recognition is rare, but, for example, most mothers can be interested in matters relating to their families, especially children. The skill of the health educator is to practise health education, in some instances without it being realized that this is what is being done. Many women read advice columns in journals and newspapers avidly, but they would not give this activity the title 'health education'. Market research shows that many men have been persuaded, mainly through advertisements, that margarine is better for them than butter, but they consider it as giving them a more manly image, rather than improving their health.

Healthier life-styles have been made possible through the use of modern materials. Nonstick frying pans and saucepans have been the largest contributors to reducing the consumption of high cholesterol fats, grills and griddles make low-fat diets an easier proposition, and their easy availability and maintenance has changed the impact and emphasis of health-education content.

Consumer attitudes are usually related to their economic and social status, they will change with time and situations. Presently there is a shift away from some of the ways of healthy living through the stringencies caused by unemployment and a tight economy. No amount of health education will overcome all the problems, but effective efforts can help to minimize them.

It must be remembered that roles of consumer and health teacher become interchangeable at regular intervals.

2. *The health worker* is assumed to be a qualified professional practitioner, predominantly with a background such as nursing, midwifery or health visiting, though the contribution of teachers and others is fully acknowledged. It is recognized that background influences practice, and that health education is not yet a profession in its own right. There are people, professional and lay, who are full-time health educators, such as health-education officers. Their tasks are diffuse and vary with geographical location. Whether health education will emerge as a profession remains to be seen, but if health education officers are effective in their roles and tasks there should come a time when they are no longer required.

Emphasis is placed on working together, being intradisciplinary, interdisciplinary and interprofessional. The mutual benefit of working in partnership in many different ways is stressed.

3. *The health teacher* is seen as teacher and learner at the same time. Teaching in this context is acknowledged to be part of a wider role, and the subject rather than teaching expertise is stressed. Some consideration is given to the tools, methods and resources which are needed for practice, and the needs of teachers and workers are recognized.

4. *Interested others*, such as politicians and advertisers, and the influences they bring to bear on health-education practice are discussed. Political awareness is recommended, and attention drawn to the levels of politics which operate within communities. The mass media, its influences and scope, are considered.

5. *New and different ways* need to be tried and evaluated. Health education is considered in the light of a process approach and other new tools, such as video games and computers, are touched upon.

Terminology

Wherever possible the use of jargon has been avoided, though it is likely that some jargon words have appeared despite this effort. A few words have been used at times and with some reluctance simply because no better or more suitable ones came to mind.

Professional refers to the practitioner of health education, who is employed and qualified to do so. No respect has been shown for the prior or additional professional role the same person may hold, such as nurse or teacher or doctor or …

Health education is seen as health teaching at all levels, ages and stages, an activity carried out for the mutual benefit of those participating in teaching and learning activities.

Recipient is the receiver of health-education messages, but not necessarily the acceptor of the message. The use of the term emphasizes the state whereby any individual will receive a multitude of information and put this into juxtaposition with knowledge and opinion already held. It hints at the possible blocks to understanding, and the individual's right to accept or reject all or part of the information received. It also hints at the distance between receiving, accepting and acting upon information. The word embodies a complex and important concept, of which health educators have to be aware.

Message is the all-embracing term used for the content of health teaching, and can be narrow or wide, general or particular. It is recognized that messages can be implicit or explicit and that they can be misinterpreted, misunderstood or create conflict. Communication is discussed in Chapter 9, but it is one of the themes running through this book.

This book draws together the threads of health education for those actively engaged in the field. However, there are distinct limitations:

1. There was constraint on space and time.

2. No one person or book can cover the wide range of the subject.

3. Decisions had to be made on what to include and what to leave out.

4. Knowledge and skills form a theme of this volume, which can only encourage their development, not be part of the active learning process and their adaptation to individual practice.

The book is meant to be enjoyed, and at the same time provide a tool for health educators to come together, to combine their efforts, and to be used by each discipline, and by a mixture of disciplines, for discussion and development of their objectives and tasks.

CHAPTER 2

DEFINITIONS AND SCOPE OF HEALTH EDUCATION

Much of the responsibility for ensuring his own good health lies with the individual. We can all influence others by our own actions.

from DHSS (1976) — Everybody's Business, HMSO Prevention and Health

Difficulties in definitions

There is no concensus regarding health education; some people firmly believe that health education, if formalized and provided without the recipients' permission, represents an intrusion into privacy. Others believe, equally firmly, that health education should be part of the learning environment of adults and the school population, i.e., that it is a matter which is important and relevant throughout life. Nevertheless attempts continue to define and redefine until objectivity and concensus are reached.

The general public regard health education as a low priority adjunct to all other things they have to cope with in daily life. Professionals, especially health and social service workers, regard it as an essential part of work with clients and patients. It is a priority in health professional education and training, and forms a large component of continuing professional education. Politicians regard it differently, according to the climate of prevailing opinion or economic and other stated or assumed needs. Recently, some politicians, some of whom subscribe to party politics and some who are active in a variety of political spheres, have acclaimed health education as a panacea which will alleviate all ills, irrespective of the framework within which health educators have to operate.

The fact that both the terms *health* and *education* can have a variety of meanings adds to the complexity of the situation and subject. These points are elaborated in later chapters and in Appendix I of this book.

The World Health Organization as early as 1969 stated the aim of health

7

education to be "... to persuade people to adopt and sustain healthful life practices, to use judiciously and wisely the health services available to them, and to make their own decisions, both individually and collectively, to improve their health status and environment".

During the same year another WHO report defined health education as follows:

> In its broadest interpretation, health education concerns all those experiences of an individual, group or community that influence beliefs, attitudes, and behaviour with respect to health, as well as the processes and efforts of producing change when this is necessary for optimal health. This all inclusive concept of health education recognises that many experiences, both positive and negative, have an impact on what an individual, group, or community thinks, feels and does about health; and it does not restrict health education to those situations in which health activities are planned or formal. In the more limited meaning, health education usually means planned or formal efforts to stimulate and provide experiences at times, in ways, and through situations leading to the development of health knowledge, attitudes and behaviour that are most conducive to the attainment of individual, group or community health.

Reports emanating from WHO since the 1960s have attempted to put the above into context and practice with the most recently stated and restated aim and objective of 'Health for all by the year 2000'. This objective has been accepted, with its implication that all facets of health education must be increased or developed, by all the member states of WHO, including the United Kingdom, and by some non-member countries, e.g. some countries in the Middle East. Whilst acceptance has increased effort and impetus, it has made definitions even more variable.

The National Health Service Acts of the United Kingdom incorporated the provision of health education as part of the prevention of ill-health, and established mechanisms of disseminating information about health topics. A duty for the provision of health education has always been explicit in the role definitions of health visitors and school nurses, and it has been implicit in the roles and functions of other health workers. NHS legislation has, however, omitted to define health education. Powers of provision within the Health Service, from 1948 to the present, have been permissive and enabling, but the exercise of these powers has varied within each of the United Kingdom countries, and within each health region or board.

Recent government reports, such as Court and Warnock, attempted to define, or stated definitions of, health, and regarded increased and improved health education as essential to achieve health. Neither Court nor

Warnock defined the terminology related to health education. Professor Court does, however, state in his report that the three commonly recognized stages of prevention, i.e., primary, secondary and tertiary, should now lead to the fourth stage, though this does not mean that the other stages can be ignored: "... the fourth preventive stage when individuals must modify their behaviour to improve their health ..." (Court Report, 1976). Professor Court bases this stage on information received from Sir George Godber, Chief Medical Officer of Health, DHSS, in an interview reported in 1976 in the 'British Medical Journal' entitled 'Building our assets'. If stage four becomes incorporated into practice, it could be seen as being entirely based on internalization, i.e., of teaching and learning, of messages leading to health-promoting behaviour, the teaching and learning taking place in phases one to three.

Individuals and organizations who contribute actively to health education, have not been any clearer in their definitions. Each has interpreted it according to the views held or the nature of the organization, each stressing the need for such an activity, the pervasiveness of the subject areas, the types of need which can be met by health education and urging flexibility in approach. This flexibility may be the real strength of health education, as it is not bounded by tradition, custom or definition.

The scope of health education

As indicated throughout this text, the scope of health education is almost limitless, confined only by the knowledge and expertise of its practitioners and constraints placed upon them. Although it is regarded with suspicion or scepticism by some of its recipients, it is nevertheless accepted as something with which one ought to be familiar, even if one ignores the obvious or implied messages provided by it. The next few paragraphs give some indication of the scope as it applies to specified practitioners; it is clearly recognized that the list could be extended tenfold, to include, for example, nurses in hospital, teachers, youth leaders and the whole range of employers who have responsibility for the health of their employees. Some of the above mentioned are, however, discussed in other chapters.

Health education within health-visiting practice

The essence of health visiting is health education. Health visitors have unequalled opportunities to be in contact with a cross-section of the total population — young parents and children, middle-aged parents and their teenagers, senior citizens, rich and poor, those apparently functioning normally and those with handicaps, individuals and groups of all natures and sizes. Health visitors have also reservoirs of knowledge and skills required to practise health education, collected through the education and training leading to general nurse, midwifery or obstetric, and health visitor qualifications, and enhanced by personal and professional experience and practice. Additionally, health visitors are generally accepted by the public with whom they come into contact, and their opinion and advice is respected, even though by encouraging individuality, independence and decisionmaking their advice may be followed in part only, or in a modified format.

All health visitors provide health education on a one-to-one basis, many are involved with small groups, and others are active in formal settings such as schools, clubs and further-education establishments. The health visitor's knowledge and skills can be enhanced by encouragement and experience. The most important factor for 'good' practice appears to be the development of confidence, as an adjunct to competence, and the recognition of limitations, and how these limitations can be decreased and overcome. A lack of confidence is often created by problems of evaluation, and the long-term, rather than immediately observable, outcomes of effective efforts. The health visitor as a health educator has been described in some detail by Strehlow (1982).

An important contribution made by many health visitors is the education in health matters of lay workers and other professionals, including medical practitioners and medical students. A function of educating other practitioners is now part of most job descriptions accepted by health visitors when they commence employment. Health centres and clinics are the scene of a fairly constant stream of professional trainees and learners of many disciplines. Whilst the scope for this professional worker is almost limitless, there are constraints of time, support — in resource and manpower terms — and the fact that health education, although a priority, is only one part of a normal workload.

Health education within school-nursing practice

Officially there have been school-nursing services for most of this century. The actuality is complex, as there are nurses employed by health authorities, nurses employed by education authorities, health visitor/school nurses, nurses responsible for one school, and nurses responsible for a range of schools as well as some other tasks in the health service. Independent and special schools may employ resident nurses, whose job description and duties may be similar to those of school nurses in the Health Service or they may bear no resemblance at all, but equate with those of a sick-bay attendant.

Initially, efforts were concentrated on improving the physical health and hygiene of school children, and eliminating infectious disease. (Elements of this remain part of the school nurse's role and functions.) This involved, and still involves, close liaison and co-operation with other workers in the public-health fields. It became apparent, even in the early days, that no amount of physical input would overcome some of the problems, unless the children and their parents understood something about their bodies, their state of health, what improvements could mean to them and how to achieve these. This could be called the birth of health education in schools.

School nurses and doctors were employed to examine and treat those children in need of treatment, to cleanse those discovered to be verminous and to provide advice and assessment for those with special needs. Though not documented in official records, the health-education input of these workers, especially nurses, increased and has continued to increase to the present day. The increase was accompanied by changing needs.

The current need for health education within schools is of a much more diffuse nature than previously, and requires enhanced professional skills, higher levels of knowledge by nurses and doctors and, above all, the ability to develop a range of personal and professional relationships with pupils and teachers. The current situation is a dynamic one. Doctors, who had opted to concentrate on a solely medical input, are realizing that the medical model of care is no longer appropriate for the 1980s, and are attempting to increase their involvement in the broader sphere of prevention and health education; nurses working within educational settings have developed unrivalled skills of dealing with and assessing the health needs of their clientele; and teachers are gaining health knowledge which they feel competent enough to impart to their students. Until the 1970s teacher training programmes did not include health subjects although newly qualified teachers may have elected to study health subjects or health education.

Parallel with changes in teacher training, resources for practising teachers increased, though these resources are not available equally throughout the country. A range of resource materials, including Schools Council Projects specially designed for educating certain age groups, are now available and accessible to many teachers.

Traditionally, the health-education component of the school curriculum was seen to fit into either physical education or biology. Enlightened schools have recognized that no one part of a school curriculum can adequately cover the range of health subjects which their pupils should know for future life and parenthood, and are making efforts to build health education into various aspects of the school day.

As teachers become more expert in teaching health matters, they also realize the limitations of their knowledge, and the role of school nurses has to be widened to encompass advising teachers on curriculum content and sources of information. The scope of school nurses, their potential as health educators, has never been fully realized, due mainly to constraints of workload, work setting and a lack of recognition of their expertise, concomitant with professional isolation. There has also been the knock-on effect of the government policy of the 1950s which stated that all school nurses should be qualified health visitors, without taking account of the already overloaded health-visiting service, the increasing needs of the school population, especially for health counselling, and the increased knowledge base underlying both health visiting and school nursing, leading to greater involvement with all aspects of the task. Latest statements issued by the DHSS envisage that each school child will have an annual health-care interview, usually carried out by the school nurse, and incorporating health education tailored to individual needs.

The scope of health education in schools is likely to increase with the implementation of the Education Act 1981, and will require constant updating of nursing knowledge, e.g., side-effects of prescribed drugs, as well as awareness of locally available resources to help all those with special needs. Health education in schools has been enhanced in recent years by the contribution of voluntary agencies and non-professional teachers. Many planned health-education programmes include representation from, for example, marriage guidance councils, family planning specialists, police officers, environmental health officers and local special interest or pressure groups. Initially it was the school nurse or health visitor, not the school teacher, who was the co-ordinator of these varied inputs and had to act as overall health educator; there has been a gradual shift with teachers taking more responsibility for the total curriculum of the class or school. In many instances the nurse's contribution and co-ordinating role remains as before or has increased. Such evidence as exists, though scanty and not well documented, appears to show that greatest success is achieved through co-operation and shared activities between teachers and nurses.

Health education within district-nursing practice

District nurses work, together with health visitors and school nurses, as members of primary health-care teams. They meet a wide range of clients and their relatives whilst carrying out their nursing duties. Increasingly their scope for health education is being recognized, and the nurse's skill in carrying out the educative aspect of the role is being included in the revised programme of qualifying education and training. Parts of the nurse's educative role have been long established, such as teaching family members to care for patients without constant and direct professional supervision, and helping the family and patient to cope with terminal illness, bereavement and long-term care. The current debate, inside and outside the nursing profession, ranges around the preventive health-education role of district nurses and the extent and level at which they are competent and enabled to carry out this facet or extension of their role. At present the reality will vary with each practitioner and with the policies of employing health authorities. It is apparent, however, that district nurses could contribute substantially to secondary and tertiary prevention by providing health education for people of all ages discharged from hospital into their care, even if the illness has been of a minor nature, for people referred to them for assessment of health needs and, above all, for the elderly population. Many district nurses are very aware of the nutritional state of their client group, of the interpretative role needed in order to enable patients to follow medical advice, of the confusion created by some prescription of medicines and a whole range of other matters with a health-education element. Many district nurses have automatically and naturally assumed the role of health educator, but others may require further encouragement and support in order to realize their full potential. The future role of district nurses is likely to include an increased preventive brief, and thereby an implicit and explicit health-education dimension. The nurse's possible contribution to the prevention of home accidents, attempted suicide, especially among the elderly and recently bereaved, and to heightening the awareness of the value of health among the population within their practice area has not yet been fully explored; the scope and potential appear to be immense. As members of primary health-care teams, district nurses may also contribute to the efforts made by colleagues, and suggest additional needs to be met, as well as participating in all phases of the health-education process.

Health education within community psychiatric nursing practice

Community psychiatric nurses are increasing in number, though their distribution is unequal throughout the health districts of the United Kingdom. Initially their role was limited to serving those patients and families referred to them by medical practitioners, including consultants, or as follow-up to inpatient treatment. Increasingly they are able to accept referral from nursing colleagues, and as their sphere of responsibility widens, their health-education role expands. Their role vis-à-vis patients and families may be very similar to that of other health workers, and represents one contribution to the sum total. Their greatest health-education scope and potential could lie in being a resource and support to professional colleagues, providing specialist information and guidance where it can be most effective. Secondly, they can achieve much by creating greater awareness among the general public about community aspects of mental health, its maintenance and how to cope with the stresses and strains of modern living. Among nurses they are also the most expert in the field of addiction, and their contribution to the prevention of addiction and its related health and social problems could be greater than it is at present. In order to be as effective as possible they need to link closely with other health workers in the community, but in some instances this is made difficult by organizational factors, such as varying work-bases, mobility, constraining policies operating within districts or units and, not least of all, a dearth of trained staff.

Health education within family planning nursing practice

Family planning nurses nowadays also work from general practice, health centre or clinic. Very often they do not become full members of the nursing or practice team, because of the nature of their sessional work. However, their health-education role would be enhanced if they worked in co-operation with other nursing colleagues. They have a very practical health-education function, subject biased, but meet many excellent opportunities for health education on a broader base. The scope of their practice could be extended or better utilized if contact with the general public was seen to be more informal and friendly, and if they were seen to use the clinic sessions and waiting areas to discuss health aspects of their work. Many could contribute, and some already do, to teaching about personal relationships. Above all they can be alert to the need for referral to other expertise available to those attending clinics. The scope within referral for health education is large; it would entail obtaining the person's consent to mention the case to a third party, and to explain and elaborate the reasons for the proposed action. The skill required to communicate appropriately, to time the suggestion so that it is educative and not intrusive, and the knowledge required to be aware of the range of possibilities necessitates the input of a qualified and experienced nurse. Family-planning nurses have only recently emerged as a professional group, with a distinct identity, and they now need to consider and determine their role and its scope.

Health education within midwifery practice

Midwives may or may not be based in the community setting, and they may or may not be in close contact or communication with above-mentioned colleagues. Which ever is the case, their educative role cannot be in doubt. The range of antenatal and parentcraft preparation, recognition of risk factors after delivery and for child development, family interactions and family planning all come within their ambit. The scope of their educative function is being extended through developments in genetics and counselling, the newer demands for pre-conceptual care and the dilemmas inherent in teenage and schoolgirl pregnancies. Because of the obvious and paramount demands of the midwifery aspects of their work, the educative elements seem to be less well developed, and are certainly less well documented. The scope and potential is likely to increase, and one has the impression of a vast untapped pool of expertise. The outcomes of their educative measures could be enhanced if they took place in partnership with other health workers, such as health visitors.

As with all the other workers mentioned, midwives often lack appropriate facilities to carry out the range of activities which are desirable. One underused facility within midwifery is the waiting area, which rarely contains any health-education materials, and which is the meeting place, often for long periods of time, for many prospective parents. Attractive posters, relevant literature and tape–slide programmes or video recordings would not require the midwife's constant presence, but could act on her behalf. Some midwives are experimenting with using varied methods of health education, especially in the general practice setting. Evidence is needed of their achievements to assist and stimulate others who may be working in less than ideal situations.

All of the health workers mentioned work from the same bases, or within defined health districts or patches. None should work in isolation from the others — the greatest scope and potential is found where there is real teamwork and where there are effective systems of communication between professionals.

Each of these workers has access to another means of health education whose scope and potential appears to be undervalued and underused, i.e., the use of the work-place as a vehicle. Few health centres, clinics, outpatient departments, waiting areas in surgeries or other communal sites carry displays of health-education messages which are attractive, relevant, accessible, current and readable. This is irrespective of the availability of such materials, and the materials and facilities could be used more effectively.

Professional health educators

As health education is one task of all health professionals, the above heading appears to be a contradiction in terms. However, there are other professional groups who have a contribution to make to health education, but who do not belong to the nursing profession. Their contribution is enhanced if it is linked with all the other efforts being made in any one locality.

Health education officers

Health education officers form a distinct element of the Health Service provision, as a result of legislation and of their own professional development during the past decade. Despite their role specification within the legislative framework, their contribution to the practice of health education at field level remains variable. Their brief appears to be to provide back-up and stimulus to existing professional health workers, to help those workers to develop their skills as health teachers and to span health-education input to health, social, education and industrial settings. They are regarded as repositories of resource materials, but are often limited in the resources they are able to provide and have insufficient materials or technical services to make the use of materials effective.

Their own professional background and bias is also variable, and may affect the way they see their role and the contribution they can make. It has been suggested that they should have a standardized form of training, or route of professional development, irrespective of whether they belonged to another profession before concentrating on health education. This proposal has yet to receive government approval or backing. Their scope is as wide as resources, including manpower, will allow. The realization of their potential may depend on the support they receive from those professional and lay workers with whom they are in contact, the policies being developed within the restructured Health Service and the economic climate which may define health education as an essential or as a luxury.

Medical practitioners

Medical practitioners are part of the Health Service provision, but not necessarily within the jurisdiction of employing authorities. General medical practitioners are mostly independent contractors, and consultants generally are partly employed within the Health Service and partly private practitioners. Medical practice should have a health-education component, but it is not always evident to those registered as patients.

One problem why the doctors' recognition of the need for health education is not matched by practice is that they rely on item-of-service for payment, and health education is not easily quantifiable in those terms. However, there are many general practitioners who support the idea of health education, and who are increasingly incorporating it into their practice and their daily consultations. A few participate in health education activities in schools, and some are involved in education through the mass media. The Royal College of General Practitioners has recently published several documents, alerting their readers, and especially members, to the importance of prevention and urging increased efforts.

There are also community physicians, whose major role is in the preventive field. Most are active in the administrative structure of health districts, and have a range of functions defined by legislation, so they can contribute little at field level. In general they support health workers carrying out health education activities, and often ensure that there is an allocation of resources for it. Other medical officers in the community health field play a varying role in health education, but are increasingly recognizing the contribution they could make.

Health education within local government services

Outside the National Health Service, but active within local government, are a variety of workers whose role and functions have large components of health education. It would be impossible to do justice to their scope within the confines of this chapter, so suffice it to mention a few:

Environmental health officers
Social workers

Teachers
Town planners and architects

At the interface between national and local health services of all kinds and providing an official consumer voice, with representation on major committees, are the Community Health Councils. Their main contribution is to make needs known, to provide information and to encourage health-education efforts when they matter most. A few CHCs have initiated local schemes, which involve a range of services including health education. They do not have a paid staff, except for the secretary, and therefore have to rely on goodwill and special interests and enthusiasm.

Outside the national or local government remit is a multitude of voluntary organizations, whose scope for health education is immense, and whose interests may be specific or general, commitment to education being whole or partial. They are too numerous to discuss in detail, but include:

The Alcohol Education Council
The National Association for Maternal and Child Welfare
The National Association for Aids for the Disabled
The Spina Bifida Association
The societies for deaf and blind people
National Children's Homes, especially their phone-in service Family
    Network
Dr Barnado's
The Samaritans
Age Concern
The Marriage Guidance Councils, Episcopalian, Catholic and Jewish

Alongside these clearly definable groups are others which have government backing, through various special interests within governments or legislation, but which are independent of government, except for the framework within which they work. Examples directly linked to health education are:

The Health and Safety Executive
The Health Education Council
The Scottish Health Education Unit

Health education also has a base in industry and commerce, through occupational-health nursing and medicine. Occupational-health nurses are qualified nurses with additional occupational-health nurse training, whose role extends over the health care and education of all categories of workers.

There is unrealized scope within the occupational-health field, partly due to lack of manpower, and partly to uneven distribution through industry. The nature of occupational-health services appears to be changing. The needs of smaller industrial concerns, industrial estates and health-service employees are being recognized and attempts made to meet those needs. In some places occupational-health nurses and those working within the primary care and community teams have established close links. In each case it appears that both groups of workers have been able to reach their objectives more easily, and that they have enhanced each other's efforts, including the provision of continuity of care of the adult working population.

The impact of health education

All the foregoing describe elements of health education which have been attempted more or less successfully. Where there has been lack of success, it does not necessarily imply lack of effect, but in many instances means a lack of evidence of evaluation, or demonstrates the shortages of resources and manpower for sustained effort.

Everyone by now is aware of the dangers of smoking or the hazards of fireworks, but many people continue to live dangerously. Perhaps the element not sufficiently recognized by health educators is the fact that some people enjoy risky behaviour, and regard it as the spice to an otherwise dull life.

The impact of health education has been lessened, because it concentrates on the negative, not the positive, enjoyable aspects of human life. Stress on more fun in healthy living, and more scope for individual freedom through good health could help educators to a higher success rate. A disapproving attitude or judgemental approach to health education appears to be counterproductive, as does extremism in the way health messages are purveyed — after all who wants to live on brown bread alone?

There are some areas in which health education impact has so far been minimal, for example, the problems of middle-life, coping with the rapid changes of modern life, effects of increased mobility and resulting loneliness. There are also areas which demand health education, but which have so far been barely touched upon, for example, the effects of unemployment, the use of increased leisure time, coping with modern technology or living in the computer age, and bridging the generation gap.

Questions relating to ethics of health education are also largely unanswered, for example: To what extent is it permissible to affect individual or group behaviour? Are professional assumptions about health behaviour valid and can they form the basis of health education practice? At what point does health education become iatrogenic and therefore dangerous?

Health education could also be used as a political tool. How far can practitioners collude in this use, and to what extent are they being used as tools, unaware of the background to the usage? Could health education be a cover-up for inaction, deliberate or accidental?

The only certainties are that health education is not a universal panacea, but that it is part of a range of professional activities, and that it has to be constantly reviewed and evaluated in order to avoid pitfalls and to create the maximum effect with limited means and minimum hazards.

Further reading

Court, D (1976) Fit for the Future, Committee of Inquiry into Child Health Services, HMSO

DHSS (1976) Prevention and Health, Everybody's Business, HMSO

1948–1981 National Health Service and Education Acts and revisions, HMSO

Report No 18 (1981) Prevention in General Medical Practice, Royal College of General Practitioners

Report No 19 (1981) Prevention of Coronary Heart Disease, Royal College of General Practitioners

SHHD/SED (1980) Towards Better Health Care for School Children in Scotland, HMSO

Strehlow, M (1980) Review, Nutritional Quarterly

Strehlow, M (1982) The health visitor as a health educator, Journal of the Institute of Health Education, 20 (2)

Warnock, M (1978) Committee of Inquiry into Services for Children with Special Educational Needs, HMSO

World Health Organization (1969) Expert Committee on Planning and Evaluation of Health Education, Technical Report Series no. 409

World Health Organization (1969) Scientific Group on Health Education, Technical Report Series no. 432

CHAPTER 3

IS HEALTH EDUCATION REALLY NECESSARY?

'Health education' are Humpty Dumpty words: whoever we are, we all think that we know what they mean, more or less, until we talk about them carefully; when that happens, we discover that agreement on their meaning, except in the most general and imprecise terms, is difficult.

from Ian Sutherland (1979) Health Education, George Allen & Unwin

The question within the chapter title is asked in order to promote debate based on reality. We, the readers and writer of this book, are obviously convinced that health education has something to contribute, or that we can contribute to others' well-being by practising it. Some would argue that it can prolong life, if tertiary prevention includes education for maintenance of health at whatever level is appropriate to the age and environment of the recipient. Others argue that it places constraints upon enjoyment of whatever is seen as a desirable life-style. Whether health education is an integral part of life — the long history of attempting to affect life-styles by health education is outlined elsewhere — or whether it is something that impinges on one's consciousness occasionally, the real objective should be to improve the quality of life, quality as seen and experienced by the consumer, patient or client not as seen by the professional. Only if this is the paramount aim, and if it is achievable in whole or in part, can professional input be justified. Within the methods used, and the planning and evaluation parts of the health-education process, consideration must be given to ethical, moral and practical issues, which will change with climates of opinion and the state of currently available knowledge.

Professional rationale for practising health education

The functions or job specification received by each caring professional upon their appointment to a particular post include, implicitly or explicitly, the task to provide health education. The implicit task has been inherent in caring for many years, but few practitioners, and most of them not until recently, have had this function stated explicitly.

Making a function explicit has not always meant that it becomes a priority or that its fulfilment is as competent as possible. Nor has it indicated that carers have been adequately prepared to carry out such functions or that encouragement by colleagues and management is of sufficient quality and quantity to enable the development of confidence and proficiency. A few examples follow to show why health education should become a conscious component for professional caring practice during the 1980s and beyond.

General nursing

General nursing requires that the patient should lead the sort of life, subsequent to his acute illness, which would prevent recurrence or deterioration, or that the patient learns to adapt to disability and dysfunction. This is based on the assumption that health is a continuum, which may at any one point require assistance, and which may also be interrupted by episodes of ill-health or disease (Figure 1).

The nurse, whether experienced or in training, is one of the health educators with many ready-made opportunities for health education. A nurse should be able to discuss, for example, diet, life-styles, medications and their side-effects, and to explain what is happening to the patient's body, how the processes of healing and repair work, and what repercussions and after-effects may be expected on body and mind. Both patient and relatives can legitimately expect a nurse to know what the effects of any treatment or care may be, how long these effects may last, what additional difficulties might be experienced and how all these could affect the way of life, work and family.

The health education aspect of general nursing is of vital importance, but it is often difficult to put into practice. It involves talking with, not at, patients and relatives and communicating on many levels. Nurses have many urgent and active tasks to perform, and may prefer to appear to be busy, so the important feature of talking with and reassuring patients and relatives is often overlooked, or even regarded with suspicion. It has been clearly demonstrated that the rate of recovery can be accelerated when full communication, and within this health education, takes place. It has also been claimed, but not proven, that actual healing occurs more speedily

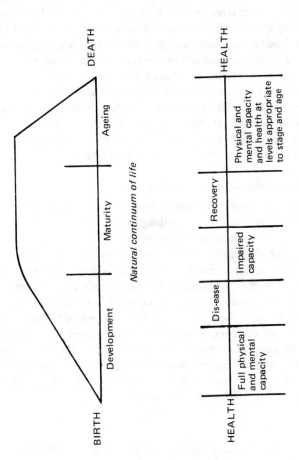

Figure 1 Continuum of Health. The Continuum may be repeated through life's phases, health education may be appropriate at any point on the scale.

when patients are fully informed about their state of current health and the progress of their illness and recovery.

Rapid recovery could mean that no sooner has a nurse got to know the patient and established a relationship than the patient is ready to leave the nurse's care, and the whole process has to be started all over again with somebody else. There have been suggestions that effective health education within nursing practice is discouraged in order to avoid too rapid a turnover of patients. Two reasons have been postulated though neither is proven: (i) that high bed occupancy and low turnover satisfies administrators who base their accounts on beds filled at certain times and (ii) to prevent nurses from demonstrating their expertise in handling information and communications so that they remain in direct contrast to medical colleagues who generally are confident in their approach to people, even when their style of communicating is actually limited and often misinterpreted or misunderstood by those not familiar with medical jargon.

Psychiatric and mental health nursing

Nurses in the psychiatric and mental health fields have become much more adept than their general nursing colleagues at communicating with people in their care. They are often reluctant to name what they do as 'health education', but the effect can be health educative par excellence. An improvement in mental health is often achieved by enabling a person or patient to express their fears and concerns, by encouraging free discussion of topics which will lead to a return to normal life at a more effective level than previously and by accepting the important task of nursing in a climate which will allow the patient to deepen and broaden their skills of daily living. Health education forms a large component of the nurse's daily work in this setting, and further improvement might be possible if the task was performed with conscious awareness, thereby increasing skilled intervention, rather than accepted as incidental.

Paediatric nursing

Paediatric nurses also communicate with their charges. They usually do this happily and willingly, and make the process of communication enjoyable. Through their obvious friendliness and care they often encourage their young patients towards healthier behaviour, and their influence lasts beyond any stay in a hospital ward. Young patients have, however, complained that nurses are reluctant to explain what is happening to them, and it would appear that a golden opportunity is being missed to help children and young people to understand their bodies, and to lead them towards better care of their bodies after they leave hospital. Many young patients are inspired to become nurses through their experience of receiving good nursing care, but few are leaving hospital better informed about health and how to maintain it.

Despite illness or discomfort most children continue to be inquisitive and curious, and are ready to learn in an informal way. The experience of being in hospital when young could be doubly rewarding if the effects lasted beyond the episode of illness to more joy in living, fewer accidents in the future, or a well-informed child, curious enough to seek further information.

School nursing

School nurses are in daily contact with children and young people. They have consistently contributed to the standards of health and hygiene achieved by a school community, but often do not appear to use the opportunities for health education which arise naturally in the school-health context. Specific and often formal contribution is made to health education or citizenship programmes, but too often the nurse remains the 'expert' visitor, who may speak on one or two topics, but who is not part of the questions and answers which may be stimulated during the subsequent weeks or months, reinforcement of teaching or follow-up to the taught subject. The school nurse's contribution should be apparent throughout school life, and affect the life beyond by stimulating a positive attitude to health, by encouraging belief in health as a valuable commodity, by explaining topics which enable healthy living and by teaching youngsters about health services, health personnel and and how to use both services and personnel appropriately.

Education for parenthood and citizenship forms part of many programmes. An important aspect of both, which comes within the nurse's ambit, is explanation of the responsibilities and pleasures of either or both, how to establish and maintain personal relationships and what effect successful relationships can have on future life. School nurses should also be available and accessible for counselling on a one-to-one basis, with self-referral by pupils, and act as an agent of referral for matters beyond her competence.

The Education Act 1981, increased the need for health-education input in schools because eventually every school and most classes will have a proportion of handicapped pupils. School nurses will be in a position to stimulate acceptance of the pupil who is different from the rest. They must also be able to explain to teachers what the particular handicapping condition means, what implications it may have for teaching and learning, whether administration of drugs is necessary, and if so, how and when this should be done, how drugs should be stored in a school or classroom, and the safety measures which might have to be taken to make integration of handicapped pupils a workable reality. The health-education role of the school nurse and her reasons for carrying out this role are obvious, and have been documented in several governmental reports, prior to the 1981 Act. The full potential of the role and function are as yet untapped.

Health visiting

Health visitors have been described as health educators with the greatest range of opportunities of doing the job efficiently and effectively. The stated aim is usually to encourage people to modify their behaviour towards healthier life-styles. It is questionable whether any professional role should actually modify behaviour, and the aim stops short of the ultimate action. The reasons why health visitors carry out their health-education functions should include:

1. Prevention of accidents, especially in the home.
2. Promotion of health knowledge, based on proven data, facts and professional experience and judgement.
3. Interpretation of health messages coming from many sources, including the mass media.
4. Providing and exchanging information, based on, for example, research findings.
5. Stimulating discussion and participation in activities leading to improved health.
6. Enabling decisionmaking in clients, decisions which can lead to better health, which are based on an awareness of all the options available, and which in their turn stimulate family awareness of health as a valuable possession.
7. Encouraging others to contribute to the health of the community.

District nursing

District nurses are in contact with people who, like the clients of health visitors and school nurses, span all social classes and age groups. In some instances their contact is fleeting, concerned with immediate, acute illness and its after-effects. In other instances their relationship with patients and their families is long term or intermittent. At a simplistic level district nurses would make their tasks much easier if they provided effective health education and thereby reduced the need for active nursing intervention. At the complex level district nurses have a responsibility to contribute actively to the health of the community by acting as health educators to patients and families, and by involvement in the health needs of their clientele in the broadest sense. They may, perhaps, achieve most if, together with other nursing colleagues, they alerted nurse managers and district management teams to the health needs of their client group and make recommendations about the most appropriate way in which those health needs could be met. All nurses, and especially those working in the community, may need to review their position, and get involved in nonnursing actions, such as representation, to improve the environment or demonstrating and documenting the health hazards of an area, housing shortages, etc.

All nurses have a teaching role in providing a learning environment for future generations of practitioners, whichever branch of nursing may become their metier. An appreciation of the value of health is the most important factor which can be taught.

Recipients of health education

Recipients may be in the settings of their own homes, schools, clubs, clinics, hospitals or any other public premises. They may be there voluntarily or involuntarily. Although teaching may be individual, in the one-to-one situation, the content of teaching is likely to be similar to more than one individual. It is, therefore, realistic to consider the recipients in terms of client groups.

Client groups may consist of individuals gathered incidentally, formal study groups or classes or any combination of these. Any group of people could be health educated, but professionals usually persuade and encourage groups to meet for the specific purpose of health teaching and learning. The group can therefore be large or small, formal or informal. The group's perspective of health education will vary considerably on a scale ranging from antipathy to the type and nature of information presented by professionals to being at the meeting place in the expectation of learning about a specific subject or range of subjects. Examples of these extremes are:

1. The health educator perceives a need of which the client group is unaware or which it regards in a different light.

2. Attendance at antenatal classes in preparation for parenthood or following an examination syllabus at school.

The middle way includes attendance at weight-reduction classes, which is normally the result of social or medical pressure and coercion, and incidental sessions such as explanations of the importance of play during developmental assessment of children.

Groups may meet because they have expressed an interest in a subject, but this does not imply that the interest is equal among its members, nor that concencus will be reached as the result of teaching.

The main reasons seen by client groups for health education are immediate application to their current state of being or need, and better use of their own resources, such as time spent caring for an ill member of their family. Secondary reasons, but still important, are a search for understanding, a desire to take the 'right' action, especially within parental roles, and knowledge of how to gain access to the best available health and medical care. Fewer client groups are interested in a community or global approach, but very often this can be generated by satisfying the first two reasons and raising interest through demonstrating the effect an individual can have on the environment and how in turn the environment affects the individual.

It is vitally important that the client group and the health educator communicate, not just talk at each other. This entails adjusting language and levels of expression, and building in a means of checking, sometimes by direct questions, sometimes more subtly, that words and ideas have the same interpretation by all present. This is not easy, as there may be regional or cultural connotations. A classic example is the use of the word 'canny' when describing a child — in the south of England it is rarely used and becomes meaningless or is interpreted as equivalent of nasty; in the northeast it is complimentary and means attractive; in Scotland it is the context that determines the meaning, which can range from lovely to sly. Another example is 'flitting' — in the northeast it means a normal move from one address to another; in the south it means leaving an address having omitted to pay rent or other bills. Use of the wrong idiom or words that are considered 'offensive' can create blocks in communication. Many recipients do not know the medical names for parts of the body, and great care has to be taken in introducing these. Words referring to the sexual organs are a case in point.

Political reasons for health education

The word 'political' may be used differently in different contexts. In this instance it is intended to be interpreted in broad, nonparty terms, although it is acknowledged that the political party and ideology in power, and the party-political system may each profoundly affect the scope, context, content and resources for health education at the time at which it is practised.

The cost of ill-health

Treatment for illness implies the use of modern technology, a battery of investigative procedures which technology and science make possible, expensive treatments and medicines, the maintenance of a system of sickness care which includes 'specialists' who can command high salaries and status and institutions with their staffs, equipment and maintenance requirements. The curative part of the National Health Service employs vast numbers of people, maintains many old and new buildings, and uses approximately 80% of all the resources allocated by government for health care. A patient's stay in hospital currently costs from £50 to £300 per day and costs related to curative care are increasing rapidly. The cost of ill-health by no means stops there. Every person, who is in paid and legitimate employment, is entitled to receive full pay or sickness benefit for the length of his absence from work. Many are in receipt of additional benefits, according to the length and nature of illness. The effects of absences from work through illness can affect business and industry, in extreme instances it can mean such loss of income or production that the livelihood of the ill person and his colleagues is permanently threatened. It has been estimated that the cost to the nation as a whole caused by sickness/absence represents a loss of between 5 and 15% of the gross national product, and thereby further reduces the possible funds available for use by the National Health Service. An ill person, though theoretically in employment, does not contribute to National Insurance payments, and is likely to benefit from a reduction in the amount of tax paid, two further reductions to the pool of available money.

Illness leading to disability, morbidity or permanent handicap increase the cost. None of the above even begin to consider the effect of ill-health on the individual and his family, the cost in human and humane terms, the volume and extent of suffering or the knock-on effect of ill-health of one member of a family, especially the spouse or other provider of care in the home, on other members. Added to personal costs must be the effect on the standard of living, if earnings are reduced by ill-health or handicap. Family expenses related to illness are rising dramatically; for example, fares to reach hospitals or surgeries, prescription charges, child-minders if visits to hospital entail long journeys or if the hospital has no crèche facility. The cost of stress and strain incurred and the long-term effects of even the shortest illness have not yet been calculated.

All the above factors have been known for many years, and most caring professionals have been concerned about some or all aspects of them. However, during a time of recession and rising unemployment, like the early 1980s, these costs can become critical political factors. There are other critical political factors, apart from allocation of resources and overt and covert governmental policies. Since 1980 up to the present (1983), and in the foreseeable future, political pressures are manifesting themselves within the Health Service in the following ways:

1. Greater emphasis on accountability.

2. Seeking demonstrable results, usually short term, without full appreciation of possible long-term consequences.

3. Demand for 'proof' of cost-effectiveness.

4. Rationalization of decisions and actions.

Pressure groups

Additionally there is the emergence of strong pressure groups, rights movements and increasing public involvement in decisionmaking processes.

There are clear indications that the nation cannot afford to continue to be generous to those in need; the rise in prescription charges is one indicator. The allocation of resources for health care are diminishing, at a time of rising costs, expenditure and need. The amount of money allocated by governments may be the same, but it has increasingly less purchasing power.

Increased morbidity

Another factor which has emerged recently, as a direct result of the current economic and employment situation, and has not yet received official recognition is the likelihood of increased morbidity among some sections of the population. This is being noticed by many health care and social workers, whose clients seek help and advice much later than is desirable in an effort to avoid such drains on personal resources as prescription charges.

Effective family planning is at risk, even for those who consider it highly desirable, as costs of supplies are increasing, and as some of these cannot be obtained on prescription. Whilst this mirrors the experience of previous periods of depression, such as the 1930s, people in 1982 have greater expectations, and different baselines for their demands. The National Health Service was formed to improve the low standards of health common in the early part of this century and it has achieved much, but it could be threatened, and change its direction so that it cannot provide the care needed by the vast majority of people, let alone better standards of health care.

Professionals, especially those within the community-health services, need to be very aware of the costs, resource allocations, and how to be 'political' in obtaining the best deal possible to help those in their care or those experiencing difficulties.

Resource allocation

The allocation of resources for curative, preventive or palliative measures is a political ploy, one rationale often quoted being 'cost-effectiveness'. Curative services are obvious, quantifiable and prestigious but their cost-effectiveness has distinct limitations. Few resource allocators have considered the side-effects, the distress or the human costs not alleviated by curative measures. Many of those discharged from institutional or specialist care have continued and still continue to require the constant attention of those working in the community and preventive fields, and, whilst no longer acutely ill, have residual illnesses of long-term duration.

There is a growing school of thought among politicians, which considers that health education can so reduce the costs of ill-health, by some magic formula which will make illnesses disappear, that all the problems of cost and resource allocation will be overcome — not in due time either, but immediately!

Ethical considerations, both of effects of illness and 'cures' or of resource allocation, have to date received scant attention. There has been some debate whether it is better to spend large sums for high-technology treatments for a few people, or the same sums on more traditional and relatively minor treatments of a far greater number of people. The debate includes the facts that the minor treatments may enable more people to function normally and happily, may lessen discomfort and pain, and may maintain strengths within the work-force; this includes housewives and mothers who, with improved health, can care for their families more adequately. The fact that high-technology treatments do not always imply a return to health, but often lead to disability or impairment of function, and that they are geographically disparate in distribution have been given insufficient attention nationally. Few nurses have actively or publicly taken part in debates on these issues, although their number is increasing. It may be that to achieve a climate for healthy living, nurses will have to become more actively involved in debates and political activities. In an ideal world all types of treatment should be available, with enough resources to employ the staff to meet all needs and demands, and research funds to continue improvements on all fronts. Utopia does not exist in the 1980s in the United Kingdom or Europe.

Political support for health education

Political support for health education provides some professional politicians with a desirable image, i.e, they appear active and concerned, and are seen to be 'doing something'. As individuals they may be genuinely caring and concerned, and have a desire to help those in need; or they may see the National Health Service as an entity to be maintained and improved, as well as believing that health education can contribute to this improvement. The relatively short politically active life of people within power structures is noteworthy, as are the means by which some seek to retain and enhance their influences. Professionals may therefore welcome the opportunity to distance themselves from political machinations, whilst using some aspects of these to the greatest advantage for the profession and clients. An open-ended approach and healthy scepticism appear a successful combination.

Most health professionals, including nurses and doctors, are employed by the state. They receive their wages from the public purse and are, therefore, part of a political system. At the same time, they are subject to various codes of ethics or practice, and have accepted the objectives and standards of their profession. One dilemma, which is becoming more acute and apparent, is, therefore, whether professionals accept and act upon political dicta, whether they attempt to change or modify the political system and decisionmaking processes, i.e., whether they get absorbed into the system as it exists, or whether they play games of politics. As an alternative, they could choose to ignore that the dilemma exists, i.e., develop the 'ostrich syndrome' or apathy. There is no easy answer. Each individual or professional group must decide the political role and stance it wishes to adopt. One requirement of the 1980s appears to be an element of flexibility, allowing adaptation to changing needs and situations. Party political affiliation is a matter for individual decision and conscience; political awareness and political action in a diversity of ways is a skill which can, and should, be utilized to advantage by each professional practitioner.

There is an official structure underpinning health education. It cannot therefore be practised without any reference to politics. Of greatest relevance are political measures as evidenced by legislation and social policy. Being within the official structure means being one cog in the machine of state. The importance and effectiveness of any particular cog depends on its mettle. No machine can function effectively if all its parts are not in their appropriate place, or maintained in good condition. One result of this is that the professional, who is part of the official structure or machine, can legitimately insist on the tools to carry out the prescribed task, e.g., resources in terms of premises, equipment, staff and appropriate remuneration. Professionals can legitimately insist that efficient and competent results can only be achieved if preparation is adequate. Such preparation may include professional qualifications, continuing education, inservice updating, knowledge of current and proposed policies, suitable information flow, as well as sufficient time to prepare for and carry out the task in hand. In turn professionals implicitly accept the rules of the structure, accountability within it and the whole range of professional responsibilities. Efforts can be made to amend or change the rules.

While it is the right of the professional to insist on the 'tools for the job', there are always practical constraints. Demands cannot be met immediately and changes have to be planned. Limited finance and resources are usually quoted as mitigating against adequate provision for professional practice. Each individual practitioner or professional group will have to decide when constraints limit their practice to such an extent that it becomes ineffective and possibly dangerous. As a result they will find the best ways and methods of overcoming dilemmas and shortfalls. Some individuals may have to decide whether to continue within the system, and accept its limitations and vagaries, or to withdraw from it.

Until the 1970s, policies relating to prevention and health education were implicit rather than explicit. The various National Health Service Acts and government circulars enabled local authorities, and later health authorities, to develop this aspect of care. Anne Lamb in her book 'Primary Health Nursing' sets out the various pieces of legislation, and how these relate to the history of professional nursing groups.

Enlightened authorities made full use of the enabling powers, and established effective services with sufficient staff. Other authorities more or less ignored those parts of the documents which were nonspecific. Many more authorities set targets for achievement, but were unable to reach the desired goals, either through lack of staff establishments, or excessive demands on their resources. Through the legislature and its officers, the government maintains a monitoring role. There is no evidence on how this operates or whether it has had any major impact.

Following the re-organization of the National Health Service in 1974, and the absorption of local authority public-health departments into the national scene, differences became obvious. In most parts of the United Kingdom attempts were made to provide a minimum standard and range of services, and plans were made to improve on the minimum. In most instances the minimum has been reached, but the rest is still to come. A few instances showed some deterioration of provision. There are many reasons for this.

Subsequent to 1974, each Area Health Authority had opportunity to appoint one or more health-education officers. The aim was to provide an impetus to health-education activities. In fact some of these posts remained unfilled for a long period, or were never advertised; some HEOs were given the scope and facilities to advance and improve health education within their area, others were appointed but constrained, and given little encouragement or facility.

In 1982, there was further restructuring of the National Health Service, and the future is very unclear. Whilst the aim is to maintain a good standard and level of services and care, including prevention and health education, there is fear that reality may show diminution and deterioration of provision.

Successive governments have stressed the need for effective health education, established working parties and supported recommendations in reports which demonstrated greater concentration of effort, but at the same time gave little guidance on how to reach targets. Many words have been written by and on behalf of governments, but few of these have been followed by action or legislation. 'Prevention and Health' was published in 1976, the first of a series; the Reallocation of Resources Working Party (RAWP) reported during the following year. The latter's suggestions were implemented, and the former was left to 'discretion'. The aim of RAWP was a levelling-out process, giving preference to parts of the country in apparently greatest need, the result, to date, appears to be an overall drop in the level of preventive provision and care.

Another classic example is the political approach to the prevention of alcohol abuse. The Advisory Committee on Alcoholism reported in 1977, and health departments, through their representatives, put considerable pressure on statutory and voluntary agencies to accept and act upon the recommendations within that report. Most professionals did accept that this represented an acute problem which required alleviation, but not at the expense of services to other equally acute and chronic needs. At the same time as the DHSS, and the equivalent departments in other United Kingdom countries, applied presssure to implement alcohol abuse prevention, another government department, the Treasury, demonstrated that it would not take measures to reduce revenue accruing from the sale of, and advertising for, products containing alcohol. In fact, access to alcoholic beverages has become progressively easier and cheaper in comparative terms. As a result, no official guidance for action was issued, and any preventive measures and education have been achieved on a voluntary basis with backhanded support from sections of the administration.

Recurrent themes

There are many questions which remain unanswered, and themes which require much more professional and public debate before concensus can be reached and effective action taken. Health education is part of the debate and any subsequent action. It is possible that there is no 'right' answer, but several relevant ones. Most of the issues are touched upon in this volume, but it is not possible to offer solutions, only suggestions. Some vital questions are posed below, and readers are invited to assist in the search for answers:

What is the real meaning of health education?
What should health education mean in the 1980s and beyond?
How much should it encompass and attempt to achieve?
Who should be called health educators?
Should such a person be professionally qualified or not?
Who should be the recipients of health messages?
Is it ethically and morally right to attempt health education, if so, what
    are the boundaries for practice?
Can health education lead to iatrogenesis?
Can health teaching be dangerous or inappropriate, even when a need is
    apparent or expressed?
Should health education be a political tool?

How can health educators avoid falling into political traps?
Should health education consist of the art of compromise, balancing
   desired goals and models against constraints?
How effective and successful can health education be at national,
   regional and local levels, taking account of the influences of mores,
   customs, religious and cultural differences?
Can an appropriate model of health education be developed, which will
   lead to effective and competent practice?

Further reading

DHSS (1976) Prevention and Health, Everybody's Business, HMSO
DHSS (1976) Report on Prevention, Advisory Committee on Alcoholism, HMSO
DHSS (1977) The Pattern and Range of Services for Problem Drinkers, HMSO
DHSS (1979) Report on Education and Training, Advisory Committee on
   Alcoholism, HMSO
Lamb, A (1977) Primary Health Nursing, Baillière Tindall
Sutherland, I (1979) Health Education, George Allen & Unwin

CHAPTER 4

HEALTH EDUCATION, AN ACCEPTABLE TASK

Teach us, oh Lord, to reverence
Committees more than commonsense
To train our minds to make no plan
And pass the baby when we can

from Anon, Hymn and Prayer for Civil Servants

Elsewhere in this book it has been stated that the words 'health education' are seen by many people as formidable, off-putting or misleading. It is suggested that the reasons for this include the dichotomy and often vagueness in the usage of the two words, as well as the low value generally given to health vis-à-vis the excitement and glamorization of ill-health. "Health is not merely the absence of disease ..." is an often quoted maxim, which has underpinned most preventive efforts during the past 30 years. However, there is still low acceptance of this in everyday life, the sort of life lived by the majority of people. Various definitions of health have been developed since the statement was first made in the 1940s but have not led to any noticeable change in the level of acceptance. As yet *health* cannot be quantified scientifically, as can signs and symptoms of ill-health; any individual's interpretation of the meaning of health may be broad or narrow, related to age and human potential or merely a reflection of that person's state of well-being at any given moment in their life.

Accepting the concept of health

The acceptance of a concept of health, with its variations according to a multiplicity of factors, is additionally hampered by the historical fact that health care, including health education, is based on a medical model, which concerns itself with systematic diagnosis and treatment, and rarely takes the whole person, his environment or total needs into account (Figure 2).

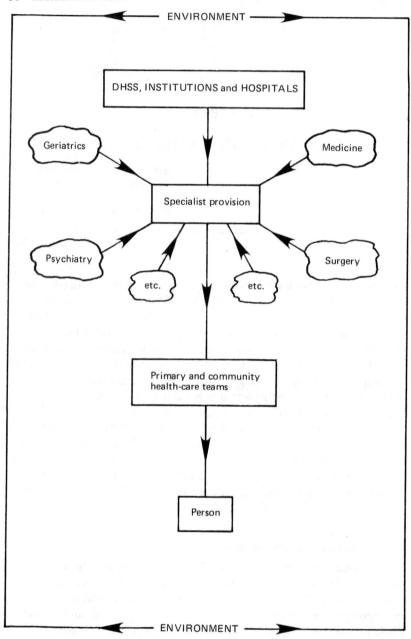

Figure 2   A model of health care

If the concept of health gains acceptance and becomes part of life, the 'treatment' required is to maintain conscious efforts to adjust life-styles so that they form a precondition for health, to practise preventive measures as a matter of routine and to review the state of well-being regularly in order that early action can be taken at the least indication of malfunction; the 'diagnosis' required includes all the known parameters which could affect health.

To achieve health the model of care moves out of the medical orbit, and is based on consideration of the whole person and his environment, his potential, his desires and ambitions as well as his immediate needs. The diagnosis would be made by each individual, with the assistance of professionals, family, neighbours and friends as appropriate.

Education has suffered from similar difficulties as described for health. Many people associate the word with unpleasant or futile experiences of childhood and adolescence. The 'good days' of school life appear to be a myth for the vast majority of people, and they are reluctant to expose themselves to any proposal which might repeat unsatisfactory experiences. The study 'Born to Fail' undertaken by the National Children's Bureau (1973) demonstrates this very clearly. In some social groups 'being educated' is a derogatory description. The initial task of any health educator is to convince the group they wish to approach that education can be painless, pleasant and worthwhile.

The practice of health education

If a sound public relations exercise precedes any planned programme of health education, it can become an acceptable practice. The public relations task would include making health a desirable goal, and education an enjoyable entity, a dialogue of teaching and learning, or a method by which the means or tools for health can be obtained. A formal approach can be counter-productive and health educators may need to utilize situations which are part of other aspects of daily life, such as advertising techniques, mass media, computers or pop culture symbols. There is as yet no evidence that videotape distribution centres include health-education materials, nor do there appear to be computer games which contain health information, although some packages and programmes with a health bias do exist. They are available to schools and are hidden within subjects such as humanities, dance, language, science or even maths.

Because of the difficulties discussed above, the search for more apt words to describe health education has had many supporters. Each suggestion has met similar snags. The 'health-education' formula has become part of professional language, jargon and an integral part of syllabuses of training for professional practice. The last decade, with its added impetus for the furtherance of health education as a professional task, the impact of this on the general public, popularization by the media and the emergence of various commercial undertakings, such as health farms, health shops, campaigns like 'Look After Yourself' run by the Health Education Council, has raised the awareness of many people of health education as an entity.

At a different level, the Open University's 'First Years of Life' and 'The Preschool Years' have not only furthered health education, but have made the idea of being part of an education system more acceptable. Through introduction to health and education by studying the above short courses, a proportion of non-professional people have continued to be interested and the Open University has fed their interest through the materials and television programmes for 'Health Choices', 'An Ageing Population' and 'The Handicapped Person in the Community'. These last can usefully form part of professional studies or a degree programme, but they appeal to a wide range of people who wish to be better informed, and through this provide improved health care for their families. The merit of the OU material is that it is as up-to-date as possible and subject to constant revision; the difficulty is that it is part of a system which seems cumbersome to many of those who would be interested. It has also become increasingly costly.

Challenges of health education

The health educator's task is not an easy one, but it is made all the more interesting by the inherent challenges. In most instances learners are well informed, whether their information is based on formal learning or experience, and whereas in the past learners were inclined to be passive recipients, they are increasingly able to express and vocalize their thoughts and ideas. One important task for the health educator is to remain open-minded and receptive, and acknowledge that health education is a two-way process. The teacher may learn extensively from the student or client group.

It has been argued that health education should be varied according to the social or cultural background of clients. The social background is likely to affect the format of health education, venues and methods of communication, but it should not create fundamental differences. The expressed needs of any client group will vary over time, and the professionally assessed needs of any community will change, but within each social group there is likely to be a compensating factor which makes the subject relevant. Whereas some client groups will have experience of being exposed to health education, or have actively sought this provision, others will be tempted to participate by the health educator, their own needs or the recommendation of friends who have had previous experience.

Any group coming together for health-education purposes is likely to have an unwritten agenda, a mental picture of what they wish to know. The experienced ones may believe that they know much already, and are likely to have previous information from many sources, including magazines and pamphlets. Inexperienced recipients may be much less confident in expressing their needs and thoughts, or consider that they know less than they actually do. Practice has shown that the two provide a balance for each other — the confident need to examine the bases of their existing knowledge, and to be led to a more critical interpretation of the information they hold; the less confident, when encouraged to express their views, are often found to possess a vast store of experience, and have learned from this. It is not easy to combine the two, but when this is possible the health educator's task is to act as catalyst and reference point, minimal additional professional input may be required. When acting as a reference point or resource person, it is important to maintain impartiality, to provide accurate and up-to-date information, and to interpret issues in the light of professional knowledge, not to be tempted to support one component of a group against the other. It is legitimate practice to express professional opinion, based on experience and judgement, as well as documented facts. The two should be clearly distinguishable.

Providing health education for a variety of cultural or religious groups poses greater dilemmas. The professionally perceived needs of these groups may be very similar to the needs of other groups, or there may be specific differences. It would be presumptuous of any professional practitioner to attempt health education with a client group if he or she had not first discovered the norms which pertain to that group. The given set of norms may include taboos, cultural and religious customs, adaptation, or lack of it, to the present environment, roles within the family and influence of other members of the group. In some instances it may only be possible to approach members of the group if the elder approves, and there may be some suspicion of any outside intervention. Sometimes outsiders, especially professionals, are regarded as a threat or even offensive, because it is regarded as proving a failure to be seen to need anything from outside the particular group. It may also be vitally important to establish whether groups are compatible with each other.

Language is recognized as a possible barrier, and the cause of much misunderstanding; however, language differences are very obvious and can be ameliorated by awareness of their complexity. Other differences are more subtle and yet more profound. One very common mistake is to take lack of understanding, through language difficulties or different sets of norms, as equivalent to lack of intelligence. This assumption is a dangerous one and can lead to a complete breakdown in communication.

Within the indigenous population of any country there are as many different cultural subgroups as those identified as specifically different through religion or cultural origins. The teenage culture of the 1970s and 1980s is very distinct from any that preceded it. Within the regions of the United Kingdom one can find a great variety of subcultures, such as the broad categories of industrial or rural societies, villages which maintain their traditions, towns where component districts or wards are based on distinct cohesive entities. Each of these will bring to the health educator a backcloth of mores, traditions and beliefs which may affect their attitudes and subsequent willingness to accept and act upon any information or knowledge. Some of these subcultures regard any person not originating from their own environment as an intruder, and will require evidence of professional capability and credibility before a productive dialogue can be started. The evidence required is not always obvious, and depends greatly on personalities, expectations and sometimes the fulfilment, or otherwise, of a stereotyped role. In some such situations the professional will always remain a stranger, but can become acceptable within defined parameters.

Language has already been mentioned in various contexts, it is a vital factor in the communication patterns of health education. Where the group, who will receive health education, and the health teacher use different languages the need for care is obvious. Not so apparent is the marginal difference in language use by similar groups. Many professionals fall unconsciously into the trap of using jargon, the in-language of their profession, thereby setting up a barrier. The barrier is often seen as a class barrier, but is in reality a misuse of common words. The use and meaning of language changes, changes and adaptations occurring more frequently and rapidly at present. Each generation has key words, which would not be used by other age groups at any price. The same word can have a multitude of meanings. Classic examples are the descriptions of illicit drugs, only a policeman on the beat or a user will know the current terminology; the change in the meaning of 'gay'; the meaning of ordinary words when used to describe the services of a prostitute or her protector; or the utilization of previously common words, such as 'memory', for new technological developments.

A task of health educators is to approach target groups because there are expressed or perceived needs — expressed by the client group and perceived by the professional, or vice versa. They may do so with confidence engendered by their professional role and functions. This is most manifest among nurses, who may or may not wear uniforms at the time. The client group may regard the educator from a very different perspective. The professional may be seen as a representative of authority, *them*, and therefore be kept at a distance, physically, socially and mentally. This view may be enhanced if the professional takes an authoritarian "I know what is best for you" stance, resulting in the acceptance of health messages in a limited, nonconstructive way only. Very often, in this situation, the impact of any health education is short term. Alternatively health educators may be seen as people, who, because of their professional background, have vested interests. Mostly in this instance the message is received with politeness, but ignored thereafter. Most constructively the health educator will be seen as an individual who is approachable, knowledgeable, experienced and caring and who will listen as well as advise or inform. Acceptance, which may necessitate explanation and description of professional roles, comes over a period of time; it is rarely an immediate event. Professional background will lend credence to any communication; effects can be short, medium or long term, and enhanced if the opportunity for reiteration and recapitulation is created. The latter is possible through regular contact, such as the routine visits of health visitors, or long-term attention of district nurses, and is an important element of the concept of continuity of care.

Consideration of the subject under discussion, by clients and groups, may be followed by partial or total acceptance of the health message, though action, such as changes of attitude and behaviour, may not always be immediate or obvious. The educator may also be seen as an individual who has a particular strength, and who is able to command attention and stimulate action, this view arising from admiration of personal or professional qualities. Such regard has positive and negative sides. It puts the onus on a person to present a constancy of approach in an equitable manner, 'slippage' can be all too easy and have long-standing effects. Professionals should be able to show that they have feelings and opinions, apart from their task orientation — in fact personal standing in the eyes of clients often rises when they realize that the professional is human, too, with feelings and failings.

Freedom of choice

'Good' practice in health education should lead to increased freedom of choice for clients. Freedom of choice is the ability to make decisions based on knowledge and a wide range of information. Health educators should be able to provide both elements. Decisionmaking processes or choices can be enabled further by providing facility for self-expression, and giving support, listening and encouragement. The ultimate aim may be to motivate towards healthier life-styles, this should not include or imply criticism of current ways of living, as these may be bounded by external circumstances which are not amenable to speedy modification. Judgements such as 'good' or 'wicked' are outside the range of successful health education, and the educator's standards and norms cannot be a guide for everybody.

In some situations where the aim may be to assist the clients to seek appropriate treatments or alternative professional advice, this can best be achieved by providing information about available choices, without emphasis on professional bias. At all times information should be as accurate as possible, in many instances requiring detailed knowledge on the part of the educator of local services, agencies and their accessibility. A careful line has to be drawn between providing information in an acceptable manner, encouraging changes in behaviour or life-style, and overstepping boundaries of personal freedom and liberty. Each individual or client group has the right to accept or reject the information and advice given, and to opt to continue to live and behave as they consider most appropriate. Behaviour which appears to an outsider, especially a biased outsider, to consist of foolish actions, or to be irresponsible, may be the only way that some individuals can cope with life. Group norms also vary and should at all times be respected. Respect shown towards different codes of behaviour and practices, even when it is clear that these are not the ones of choice of the professional, create respect in return. In some instances the creation of respect for behaviour which is outside the norms of the client group, may be a most effective form of community education, closely linked with raising health standards. An example is the expression of affection or welcome amongst different groups. There are those who consider touching each other offensive or for whom it is taboo, and those to whom it is a natural form of expression, ranging from handshakes to embraces. Females within some groups are reared to avoid the attentions or ministration of males, except husband or father, and therefore may require a different approach from caring personnel or neighbours within any setting.

Dietary practices are another example, causing suspicions and mockery among the uninitiated. Understanding the reasons and rationale for food taboos and differing methods of food preparation can raise the level of interaction within a community, as well as ensuring that nutritional levels are maintained or improved within varying groups.

Violent or nonviolent behaviour can also be part of group norms. Understanding when violence, in word or deed, is 'normal', such as, e.g., verbal aggression among some teenagers, and being conscious of the boundaries of group norms can help to contain and diffuse potentially harmful situations.

Professional practitioners may act, and be seen to act, in certain ways, such as a reluctance to communicate personal information, and an unemotional approach to very emotive situations or their particular style of practice. Explanation of professional group norms, rationale for confidentiality of some information and the experience and background which may lead a professional to regard a situation in a different light to the clients can create understanding followed by acceptance and respect.

Overcoming the barriers

Most barriers to successful health education can be overcome with time and effort, but first they must be recognized and analysed by the practitioner. Recognized, so that they do not become entrenched attitudes of educator and learner, and analysed as part of the process of the task, so that a conscious effort can be made to build bridges across the barriers. The simile of building bridges is an apt one, time is essential to achieve a coming together, to allow learning to take place.

Professionals can be creators of barriers, by distancing themselves from the situation and clientele, by showing bias or by being found lacking in knowledge or relevant experience. Clients, especially young clients or children, are very quick to detect the person who is not sincere. They are usually willing to consider any point of view, if it is genuine. No professional can possess such expertise that they can provide the answer to every situation or question. One barrier-breaker is to admit a lack where it exists, but to ensure that the gap is filled as quickly as possible. Honesty in approach, a tolerant outlook and willingness to consider opposing points of view are the quickest way to break down barriers. Honesty is not easy, as many professionals are trained to dissemble, and admission of a gap in knowledge is regarded as equivalent to failure by some people. Nurses, especially those who completed their qualifications some time ago, were professionally reared to adopt an authoritarian approach, and to pretend that they are competent at all things. It requires knowledge of self to break the mould. Every nurse should remain an authority on health matters, but teaching of these matters can be relaxed.

Any client group or individual client is likely to have expressed needs or interests, which may differ from those of health educators. Success is more likely if the process of teaching and learning starts from the expressed, and therefore paramount, concerns and moves from this base to other areas. The movement will sometimes be rapid, at other times excruciatingly slow. Moving from the known to the unknown provides the comfort of familiarity, and allows people to cope with ideas which may be new and alien. Programmes for ongoing health education are best evolved in partnership between clients and professionals. Enabling clients to become integral parts of the process creates feelings of achievement and confidence to experiment with new and different ways and ideas. There is a fear among many professionals that when using the partnership approach they may lose control of the situation. Partnership implies an egalitarian way of working, which gives full credit to clients' freedom of choice, and alters the traditional, authoritarian stance of many practitioners. It may require adaptation in practice and a review of personal attitudes which can be difficult and painful. However, the results achieved on personal and professional levels appear to make the attempt and effort worth while — in many instances a sharing of 'control' leads to greater acceptance of professional expertise and enhancement of professional skills.

Health education is one large concept, within it there are many components representing a range of other concepts. 'To conceptualize' means to understand, not only facts, but how facts relate to each other, and how given sets of facts fit into a theoretical framework. Theoretical frameworks may be based on evidence provided by research or other documentation, or on ideals and philosophies. Considering a subject and its component topics through the medium of concepts does broaden the bases, it provides facility to look at issues surrounding topics and to incorporate many different aspects, standpoints and expertises. It usually leads to discussion of related issues and stimulates active participation and fruitful debate. Health issues are rarely simple, and their complexity is due to the interrelationship between health, environment, housing, work, living standards, beliefs, customs and values. Complexity is compounded by rapid changes in one or more of the factors. Health educators may feel that they have to deal in broad concepts when discussing health issues. It is not clear, from existing evidence, whether it is more beneficial to move from broad concepts to details or vice versa. The majority of client groups are likely to prefer consideration of particular aspects and move from those into the range of concepts relating to the matter in hand. It becomes progressively easier to move from one concept to another. A few examples are:

1. The subject of infant feeding may be the paramount concern of the client group. Through discussion of this, nutritional principles can be extracted and developed, relating to individuals of different ages, to families with differing component needs, to the community in which clients live and to the nation and, lastly, to the world. The last three aspects have to consider many different concepts, facts and ideals.

2. The subject may be 'health as a desirable goal', incorporating the value of health, what it could mean to different individuals within the group, the group as a whole and families and the community. It should lead to consideration of various aspects of health, health maintenance, how to cope with ill-health, abuses and addictions, influences on health ranging from personal budgeting to political pressures. Some parts of this will be known by members of the client group, but would lead to consideration of other, unfamiliar topics, ideas and concepts.

3. Child rearing is a subject of interest to most parents, and often grandparents and parents-to-be. Its teaching would include the familiar patterns of the neighbourhood in which the client group lives, health-care provison and policies, schooling and youth employment, teenage needs and cultures, parent expectations, human development and the range of normality, research evidence related to the subject and legislation affecting parents and children. It may lead to discussion of women's roles, male domination, changes in either and how these affect child-rearing patterns, day care provision and marriage, partnerships, divorce and the whole range of human relationships.

Few health educators will have the opportunity to cover the whole range of topics and concepts related to a subject, as this would have to be developed through repeated contact and would require time. Priorities will have to be decided, and the most relevant extracted, indications of the range should, however, be included in any programme.

Success may be assessed through evaluation, a process approach or by the expressed demand for continuation, extension of contact or evidence that alternative means of learning have been sought. It may be impossible to meet all requests received, needs identified or stated demands; the fact that a dialogue or debate has been started should suggest that the practice of health education has become acceptable to the community served, or to the original target group.

Further reading

Boswell, D (1974) The Handicapped Person in the Community, a reader and source book, course P853, Open University & Tavistock Publications

Carver, V (1978) An Ageing Population, a reader and source book, Open University

James, M and Jongeward, D (1975) Born to Win, Addison Wesley

Open University (1980) Good Health Guide, and resource pack, Open University & Harper & Row

Perkins, E (1979) The case of the Open University parenthood courses, Occ. Paper No. 12, Networks and Dissemination, Leverhulme Health Education Project/ Nottingham University

Wedge, P (1973) Born to Fail, National Children's Bureau

Open University Courses

Health Choices, course P921

The First Years of Life, course P911

The Pre-school Child, course P912

CHAPTER 5

HEALTH EDUCATION AS A PROFESSIONAL SKILL

Great things are done when men and mountains meet
This is not done by jostling in the street

from 'Great Things', William Blake

Professional people are usually proud and possessive of the range of skills they possess, especially those skills which are specific to their professional practice. Lawyers jealously guard their prerogative to argue difficult legal matters, politicians to make laws, doctors to legitimize sickness and skilled craftsmen to produce certain goods or services.

Nurses are skilled practitioners in the care of people. Some have specialized to care for groups with specific needs, some to practise their skills in an institutional or hospital setting, and others to care for people within a community or district. Nurses, social workers and teachers general medical practitioners and midwives may care for the same client group, each having distinct roles and functions to perform in relation to the clientele and each conforming to the prescribed parameters of their professional ethos.

Human needs do not easily accommodate to or recognize professional boundaries; all caring practitioners have some areas of role overlap, and it is not always clear who may be the most appropriate person to provide the care at a given time. Teamwork can provide a solution to this, and avoid wasting time and resources, as well as preventing confusion in the minds of clients as to whom to contact at times of stress or need. Professional boundaries can be used by clients to play games with professional resources and to use the words and actions of one health worker to galvanize another. 'The games people play' are not confined to those described in Berne's book, but can have limitless variations.

Health education is at the crossroads of professional practice, with few practitioners having a total commitment to it, but many having it incorporated into their functions. Health-education officers may consider

49

themselves the only whole-time professionals in this field, with full commitment to the development of health-education practice theory and special skills. This could be challenged and questioned. Some health-education officers do have sufficient skills and experience to be regarded in this way, whereas others have constraints placed upon them. Taken as a whole, health education has some way to go before it can claim to be a professional practice in its own right, if it ever does so. It may not be in the best interests of the field and its consumers to be seen as a separate entity, divorced from other forms of health care or education.

Most caring professionals, nurses, doctors, therapists and some of their qualified assistants have a duty to practise health education as part of their professional range of tasks. The major professional skills will have been acquired during training prior to qualification, but skills for health teaching are likely to have been a secondary consideration and therefore incorporated only briefly or superficially. It does not appear that the skills of nursing, medicine, teaching or social work automatically prepare a person to be skilful at teaching health. Therefore, there are two paramount issues to be resolved; first, is health education a professional skill; if not, what is it?, and, second, if health education is a professional skill, how can this be learned, and once learned, maintained and improved?

It must be accepted that, whilst the practice of health education is one professional skill, nonprofessional people often engage in the same activity with considerable success. Nonprofessionals have an advantage in that they do not have to consider rules and regulations of professional practice, and can, therefore, give full rein to their enthusiasms. It is sometimes disturbing to find that an enthusiastic amateur can be successful where professionals have not achieved their set objectives. However, professionals have the advantage that practice must continue as long as there is a proven need and as long as the professional practitioner carries out a caring role, whereas the amateur may decide at any time that there should be a change in their activities or that they become interested in something very different, perhaps even leading in the opposite direction to health education.

Contributory skills

So far health education has been considered as one skill for the professional practitioner. It is more likely to consist of a number of skills, put together to make a pattern for practice. The component skills needed to make the grand total include:

1. Communication by a variety of means, methods and at different levels.
2. Listening.
3. Ability to assess needs, on an individual and a broad basis.
4. Willingness to search out health needs.
5. Presentation of self and subject in an acceptable manner.
6. Awareness of climate of opinion, fashion and changes.
7. Manipulation of the environment to make it a suitable medium for teaching and learning.
8. Creating an atmosphere conducive to open-ended learning.
9. Being approachable, honest and free from prejudice whilst maintaining professional standing and standards.
10. Adaptability to a variety of situations and conditions.
11. Ability to cope with constant change.

The above list of skills could be enlarged, but these appear to be the most important ones for the 1980s. Some of them may be innate, and require very little in the form of formal training to develop. Most nurses, because they care for people in the general sense rather than professionally or physically, have these skills latent within their natures. Increased self-awareness will differentiate those skills which are part of a person, and those which have to be acquired. In each instance the innate skills can be enhanced through training and experience. Nurse education does relatively little to further the necessary skills, though elements of health education are included in the syllabus of training. However, nurse education does provide skills of observation, analysis and evaluation which create competence and confidence in nursing practice, and which require minimal modification to lead to successful health-education practice. A background of professional nursing experience and training should also provide the basis for developing communication skills.

Nurses working in the community, whether they are health visitors, district nurses, midwives or school nurses, have normally received postregistration training, which will have enabled development of the skills needed to practise health education. All groups of nurses working in the community act as health educators to individual patients or clients, and become extremely skilled in the educative function of their role in the setting of people's homes, clinics or treatment rooms and school medical facilities. They are often hesitant to practise in alien or more formal settings. The skills needed are no different, whether the setting is familiar and comfortable, or strange and relatively stressful. All nurses, with postregistration expertise, have the ability to carry out health education at most levels, their greatest need is to develop self-confidence and practical experience, enhanced by support and encouragement.

A deviation, though not an exception, from this is the health-education function of health visitors and school nurses within educational settings, where their health-education practice has to be able to stand the test of professional educators and complement it. Confidence in their own ability and the assurance that their knowledge base is sound are the criteria to use. Education is only one part of their total role, whereas it is the teachers' raison d'être, therefore they should be fully aware that they are not in competition with teachers, but that they remain the experts in health subjects. Collaboration with teachers in planning any programme, and co-operation in providing the follow-up, can lead to a great measure of success. An additional skill required by health visitors and school nurses who become very involved in the health-education programme of one or more schools, is 'crowd' control. Children and adolescents do respond to teaching, but they are often not in the classroom by choice, and may become restless. There is also the fact that any group of school pupils will be at differing stages of emotional development and respond to teaching about health according to the stage reached. Most youngsters, whether they openly admit it or not, are fascinated by their bodies and its functions and by interpersonal relationships. They are also interested in the effect they can have on the world outside the classroom, and are likely to be more interested in those aspects of health which give them the ability or prowess to shine outside school. They will often 'test' the teacher, by throwing questions designed to embarrass or show the teacher's gap in knowledge, but will respond rapidly if the 'test' is passed, i.e., no embarrassment shown and honest answers given. There may be occasions when the health expert has to say "I don't know" or "I am not willing to discuss this subject". To be able to say this with confidence and to pass on smoothly to the planned subject area is a skill acquired only be repetition and experience.

Acquiring the skills

There are two main ways whereby those teaching in formal or educational settings can acquire the necessary skills to enhance those from their nursing and postregistration trainings. One is through continuing education provided in the further and higher education systems, and the other is through their employers by programmes of inservice training. The most useful courses within institutions of further or higher education are the multidisciplinary health-education certificate courses, validated by the Health Education Council and the City and Guilds Teachers Certificate. These may be provided on a part-time or day-release pattern, so making it possible for those in employment to attend. They are not expensive, though there is a cost factor in the purchase of books, course fees and travelling expenses. These courses are not regarded as an additional professional qualification, but they can enhance professional expertise and standing. In some parts of the country other courses are offered, but local knowledge is required to pinpoint where these are and to establish their content and usefulness for practice.

The majority of employing health authorities regard such programmes of training as staff development and encourage attendance, though in the present climate of financial stringency a clear case has to be made by the practitioner when applying for release to attend courses. Requests for release have to be made approximately 1 year in advance of actually attending a course, to allow budgeting for relief staff or contribution to fees.

Some employing authorities provide programmes of inservice training, specially designed to enhance a range of skills. These have increased in recent years both in availability and quality of content. Other authorities circulate information about available study facilities outside the immediate jurisdiction of the authority, but giving practitioners the opportunity to participate. Some of these are extremely worthwhile.

Each Local Education Authority provides the facility of a Teachers' Centre, which usually houses educational materials and is a meeting point for teachers from many schools. Those practitioners providing health education in schools are likely to be made welcome and able to benefit from this type of informal continuing education. Some Teachers' Centres have organized seminars or occasionally invite outside lecturers on subjects of current topicality or relating to the processes of education. This could be another easily available source of increasing skills in teaching health subjects.

Few practitioners, and none of the nursing groups, practise in isolation, though some may have closer proximity to colleagues than others. Another way of enhancing skill is to utilize the resources provided by professional colleagues. Peer-group support or self-help can be one of the best and most appropriate ways of professional development. The self-help group may consist of professionals from one discipline, and be totally self-reliant, or it may draw on outside expertise. Alternatively it may be an interdisciplinary group and consist of various groups of nurses, for example, those working in a primary care or educational team. It could also be multidisciplinary utilizing expertise of many of the caring professionals in any given geographical area. Self-help groups are often underestimated in their possible impact, because, taken at face value, they are the least expensive to run. However, they can make a significant contribution to effective practice, and should at least be given the resources, such as use of premises and time to carry out their activities. Self-audit is becoming the norm in some professions, and contact as described above can assist practitioners in developing the skills of audit, especially as this relates to their own practice.

Knowledge base

Successful health education relies not only on skills of practitioners, but also on the assurance that practice arises out of a sound knowledge base. All nurses will have a knowledge base from their basic training programmes. However, even for those who followed the same syllabus, the actual knowledge may vary in breadth and depth. Some will have forgotten through lack of use, others will have forgotten some of the basic information but replaced it by newer or more recent knowledge, still others will have gaps in knowledge which have always existed, and of which they are unaware. The most efficient and competent practitioners will be very aware that the knowledge base is shifting constantly, and that part of their personal professional responsibility is to maintain and improve the base from which they work, and make efforts to cope with constant shifts and changes.

Professional journals abound, providing relevant information which could become knowledge; few people can afford the time or money to read them all. Awareness of what they contain is necessary for maintenance of competence in professional roles and functions. A self-help situation can be contrived whereby individuals take responsibility for reading one or more journals and alert colleagues to relevant content. Another way is to scan a range of journals in libraries, public, nursing and medical, and extract copies of relevant articles. Copyright allows one or two copies to be taken for educational purposes, but not sufficient for circulation. It is an effective mechanism, but requires time. In some health authorities nursing officers have made it their responsibility to alert their staffs to relevant published material. This is a very welcome and positive development, but in the long term no professional practitioner can rely on another to provide the stimulus, and has to accept that keeping up-to-date is one part of the job.

Many health authorities do provide specialist libraries, access to relevant information or access for all practitioners to libraries sited in schools of nursing or medicine. Organizations such as the Health Visitors Association and the Royal College of Nursing enable easy access to a wide range of written materials, especially newly published books. The RCN library is one of the most comprehensive on nursing and health matters. The HVA additionally publishes a 'Current Awareness Bulletin'. The Health Education Council makes subject-specific material readily available. In each instance the information can be obtained by personal or postal application.

Another aspect of professional responsibility, which often becomes blurred in practice, is to determine the knowledge needed for competent practice of the role and functions for which one is employed, rather than absorb a range of interesting information which becomes constantly available. It is human nature to be curious and interested in matters outside one's immediate ambit, but when there are constant demands on time and skill it may be essential to establish priorities even in the acquisition of knowledge. In an ideal world each professional would have the opportunity to take regular sabbatical leave from their job to undertake reading and studies, both of professional and general interest. Nurses working in the community, and especially those acting as health educators, have an especially onerous task relating to the knowledge they require for practice. They have to possess sound, up-to-date knowledge of nursing skills and procedures, an awareness of developments in medicine and how these are likely to affect nursing practice, knowledge of social policy and how this affects practice and the life of their patients and clients, changes in policies and legislation, knowledge of human behaviour in practical, sociological and psychological terms, and an awareness of the knowledge and levels of understanding within their client groups. Additionally they have to be a fount of local wisdom, where to find whom and what, and be able to discuss local as well as national and world events as reported in the mass media with clients.

When listed all this sounds impossible to achieve, but, in fact, as some of the knowledge becomes absorbed by the person, the acquisition of additional information acts as a stimulant. The range of knowledge needed is a challenge to be welcomed. The most complex aspect of the acquisition and retention of knowledge is to phase it, so that it becomes an enjoyable process, and a useful habit, not a matter for stress and strain.

Professional practitioners should be able to assess which aspects of additional information they are unable to obtain by self-help, and to discuss with colleagues and managers how best to overcome any deficiency. Deficiency in this sense is not perjorative, but is a facet of professional development which occurs regularly. It appears to occur more frequently in the rapidly changing world of the 1980s. It is fully recognized that any professional, who is to maintain professional standards and remain a safe practitioner, will need continuing education throughout professional life. This may take many forms, from refresher courses to advanced or degree studies, through studies of specific topics, and occasionally requiring a whole new and different orientation. Employers have a responsibility to provide sufficient means of continuing education to lead to safe practice; practitioners have a responsibility to recognize any shortfall and seek the most appropriate means of overcoming this.

Since the 1970s, most nurses have been subject to 'performance review', and doctors have largely moved towards self-audit. At best either scheme can provide the tools to assess the state of current awareness and knowledge, and suggest the means for filling any gaps, at worst either scheme can set up blocks of resentment. Both can be useful tools when used well, but they are tools and do not replace the personal, professionally orientated approach.

Attitudes

Any educationalist would refuse to consider skills and knowledge, without taking account of attitudes. Attitudes are discussed in other chapters in relation to client groups and subject matter, but in this context there are a few points which appear of major importance.

Honesty of approach has been mentioned. This may necessitate the awareness that a particular facet of health education is 'out of bounds' for the health educator, because his own attitude would preclude an unbiased approach. Awareness of personal biases or prejudices is fundamental to 'good' practice. Awareness can allow effective health-education practice, even if an attitude, bias or prejudice precludes a person from dealing personally with a topic, subject or group. Self-awareness may lead the health educator to persuade a colleague to help with the practice, or to attempt to overcome the difficulties. Ideally a professional person should be able to overcome biases and prejudices, but in practice some of these may be so deeply rooted that it may be foolish to attempt a change. Bias or prejudice may be towards a subject, for example, family-planning methods, or towards a particular group, such as a religious sect. Nurses' responsibility, and especially those working in the community setting, is towards all equally, therefore this can become very important. It has also been noted that levels of tolerance change with age and experience, from the intolerance of youth to the intolerance of age, with various degrees in the intervening years. Nurses and other caring professionals are not immune to these changes, but may be able to overcome them with experience and awareness. Prejudice and bias can, of course, be positive as well as negative, each carrying hazards, the one of overenthusiasm, the other of apathy.

Attitude change is talked about as though it was an easy matter. However, most attitudes are formed quite early in life, and are dependent on a variety of influences — parental, social, environmental and educational among others. To change or influence a person's attitudes takes time, patience and perseverance, and care has to be taken that the replacement attitude is not equally undesirable. One objective of health education, both for the client and for the professional, may be attitude change; the important precursor to change would appear to be attitude awareness, followed by modification rather than complete change. Only when consensus has been reached and awareness is total, can attitudes be really changed. Any change may still be suspect, as it can be subject to other influences and may vacillate for a considerable length of time.

The skills, knowledge and attitudes brought to achieve successful health education vary with each practitioner, and depend on experience, the nature of professional background and qualifications, and the current situation in which health education is practised, for example, adequacy or otherwise of accommodation and constraints placed upon the practitioner. Each professional will bring some unique skills and knowledge to the task, attitudes may be individual or collective, ability to practise may range from very limited to extensive, all making the nature and extent of health education flexible and variable.

It has already been said that health education, by its very nature, cannot be the prerogative of any one profession, and that nonprofessionals may have a substantial contribution to make. Success is increased if health education occurs in partnership with client groups, or, if necessary, in collusion with part of a group. It is not clear, because there is no substantive evidence, whether success is greater if each professional makes their contribution in an individualistic manner, or if the variety of contributions are mixed in practice, the overall approach is multidisciplinary, or a mixture of professional and lay. The latter has proved very successful in the case of encouraging breast-feeding, by using health visitors and midwives as one side of the health-education team and the Natural Childbirth Trust and Laleche League as the other. Possible permutations are limitless and appear to indicate that a flexible approach and the willingness to seek the most appropriate means for any given situation is the most practical and realistic. Most health-education outcomes can only be assessed subjectively, as the objectives for health education are usually broad, and some results may only manifest themselves in the long term. There is, for example, as yet no answer to whether those children who have received parentcraft education in schools actually prove to be better parents, or how improvements can be measured. Many objectives of health education are based on values such as 'improved' or 'better', and it is rarely clear whether the values are common to recipient and health teacher, or to what extent improvement is the result of health education or other factors.

As a professional practitioner, one is usually required to be able to justify one's activities, and to make a statement about their outcomes. There is a need, therefore, to move towards some form of evaluation of health-education activities. One way of evaluating could be to formulate objectives for each programme and behavioural objectives for each session and its component parts. Means could then be devised to measure to what extent objectives have been achieved, whether the educator reached the targets set, and whether the recipients considered that there was potential for them in health education. The person doing the measuring could be the health educator, a colleague, a manager, another health educator, a member of the group or a member of the general public. A formal evaluation process would be helpful in policy and planning, may lead to improved resources, and if the results are analysed and shared with others, it could lead to more effective health education. Analysis should look for the factors leading to success or failure. However, to establish such a process would require additional skills, knowledge of handling statistics and an attitude which saw health education as an integral part of the health service. Some tools of measurement are likely to prove helpful for future individual practice, but it would appear that a formalized process of evaluation can act as an inhibiting factor. The greatest measure of success would appear to be increased demand for health professional input, by colleagues from other disciplines as well as by client groups, increased confidence in the ability to carry out the task, increased enthusiasm, evidence of teamwork or partnership and enjoyment by educator and clients in working together towards agreed goals.

This does not absolve professionals from the responsibility of reviewing their position and perspective at regular intervals, and to seek to increase their levels of effectiveness and competence in practice. A study undertaken in south Glamorgan among some practitioners showed that they were doing their jobs reasonably competently, but that once the job had been analysed and reviewed they were enabled to perform very much better.

Further reading

Baly, M E (1975) Professional Responsibility, HM&M

Berne, E (1964) The Games People Play, Penguin

Brown, F (1982) Health education in nursing, Nurse Education Today 2(2):21

Chisholm, M K (1981) Health education in nursing practice, Midwife, Health Visitor and Community Nurse 17(12):505–506

Davies, A (1980) The changing nature of health education, Nursing Times, Oct. 23, 1890

Ellis, R and Whittingham, D, (1981) A Guide to Social Skills Training, Croom Helm

HEC (1980) Health Education in Nursing, a survey of nursing in England, Wales and Northern Ireland

Smith, J P (1977) The progress of health education, Nursing Mirror, March 24, 39–40

Useful addresses

The Royal College of Nursing Library, Henrietta Place, Cavendish Square, London WC1

The Health Visitors' Association Library, 36 Eccleston Square, London SW1. 'Current Awareness Bulletin' available regularly by subscription.

The Health Education Council, Publications Department, 78 New Oxford Street, London W1

CHAPTER 6

THE HEALTH-EDUCATION PROCESS

Skilled work gives us some unusual insights into how the worker becomes limited and dominated by the work process.

Harley Sheiken (1977) in Illich, I et al. (1977) Disabling Professions, Marion Boyars

The meaning and importance of health education has been discussed in previous chapters, both explicitly and implicitly. The practice of health education will be considered at some length in subsequent chapters. There is, however, a need to consider whether there is a theoretical basis for health education.

It is clear that there is no unique basis of knowledge which will enable a person to become a health educator, rather it is an amalgam and extraction from a variety of knowledge bases, for example, biology, history, nutrition, educational theory, philosophy and methodology. One attempt at providing a theoretical framework was made in the book 'Health Education' (1979) edited by Ian Sutherland, Director of Education of the Health Education Council. The varied contributions in the one book demonstrate the complexity very clearly.

Nursing process

In contrast, nursing, and especially all aspects of public-health nursing, has added a unique body of knowledge to the amalgam of theoretical bases which leads to the application of caring for individuals and groups in health and sickness, and which has most recently been interpreted in terms of the nursing process. The nursing process was first defined in the USA, but has become accepted practice in other English-speaking countries. It was defined in 1968 as "assisting individuals of any group to meet their basic human needs in coping with their health status at some particular point in their life cycle".

There appears to be a concensus that health education is a part of nursing. It is a major component of all public health work, health visiting, school, district and community psychiatric nursing. The nursing process could be transposed to health education, either as part of the application of the existing process or as a whole.

Before considering the components of a health-education process, practitioners need to understand the currency of the nursing process. The concept was imported from the United States some 10–15 years ago, and has gradually gained momentum in Britain. Its major aim is to lead to effective 'total patient care'. Much has been written about the nursing process, but the conflicting descriptions and scanty evidence have led to some confusion and difficulty in assessing the validity of a process approach. Evidence of its successful application is now accumulating, and there is less resistance to its wide application. The initial writings often obscured the goal and method by wrapping the concept in jargon; American practice was not always seen as relevant to the British way of life and work. However, now the writings are applied to local situations, and shown to be relevant to nursing care within the National Health Service.

Total patient care is a desirable goal, eliminating the dangers of considering a person as only possessing malfunctioning parts, and accepting the patient's stay in hospitals or institutions as the temporary episode it usually is. As practised in most places at present, the application of the nursing process can lead to more effective, improved nursing care. The ideal will not be completely achieved until doctors, nurses, therapists, dieticians and all other members of caring professions move much closer than at present to a full team approach to care.

The nursing process is being used in many institutions and settings, both as a means of achieving the goal of total patient care and as a tool for teaching the care of individuals within their environments. The application of the nursing process is being tested in nursing situations outside institutions, and many professionals are endeavouring to make it a workable reality. The process approach is being applied in district nursing and health visiting, although not as yet in all practice areas. The process may need some modification to be fully applicable to any public health practice, but this proves it to be a valid and dynamic idea, a framework which can be used and applied to any caring situation. Ann Hendy, at the 1982 annual conference of the Health Visitors Association ably described the process in health-visiting practice, and urged its acceptance on a much wider scale than at present.

There are still some practitioners who are sceptical about a process approach, and some who remain unconvinced and do not consider that this is a valuable or appropriate method of caring for people. There is a distinct hazard in the approach, which does not detract from its value, that it could be regarded as a means or an end in itself, forgetting that it is a tool for achieving a wider aim. It can also be misapplied, and thereby rendered ineffective.

The nursing process has been described as a useful tool, a means of achieving better care. It can also be considered as a philosophy of caring appropriate to the twentieth century, bringing job satisfaction to care providers, and giving assurance of the best possible care for those in need of it, i.e., the consumer or recipient.

A process approach has been tried and tested in industry and commerce for many years and found to be the only sure road to success as demonstrated in annual reports of successful companies, e.g., B.P., LASMO and BBC computers. A process, whether it applies to human beings or to manufactured goods, is a means of achieving maximum success with minimum waste and effort, using logical steps in forming and reaching goals, or, as defined by the 'Oxford Dictionary' 'a course of progress'.

When the steps of any process, namely,

1. assessment of the situation, data collection;
2. analysis and plan of action;
3. action according to plan, by one or more persons;
4. evaluation of progress and outcomes;
5. assessment and modification taking account of evaluation, new data and incomplete planned actions;

are applied to human conditions, allowances have to be made for all the factors, or as many as one can reasonably calculate, relating to individual differences between receivers and providers of care. The processors have to take account of the major factor that humans are not subject to realistic, or infallible mechanical tests, and are capable of interpreting information and knowledge in a variety of ways. Because of this, the application of any process to people of any age has to be considered as an interlocking device, the initial assessment being allied to and overlapping with final evaluation. It must also be considered as a continuum, used for planning the immediate — for example, a teaching session for tomorrow afternoon — and the long

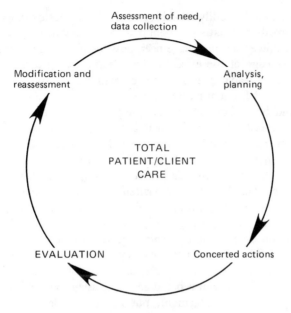

Figure 3   A process approach

term — for example, the health care of a community with its changing composition and needs.

In the same way as the nursing process can lead to improved nursing care, and ultimately to total patient care, so a health-education process can lead to improved practice and better results, provided that realities are kept firmly in view (Figure 3). The following attempt to outline a process approach to health education has the aim of providing an aid to practitioners, avoiding the evident pitfalls in the hope that practice will lead to refinement of the idea, and the formulation of an appropriate and realistic philosophy.

Assessment of the situation and data collection

For the provision of effective health education, this phase of the process has to have three component parts:

1. Collection of data.
2. Assessment of need.
3. Assessment of available resources, including people and time.

The data is generally readily available and can demonstrate a range of needs. There are broad-scale statistics about preventable accidents at work, home and school. Prevention may have been possible if those involved had had greater knowledge of the effects of their actions or inactions. There is evidence of the spread of preventable body malfunction, such as obesity and smoking-induced bronchitis, which require education towards changing attitudes and behaviour. There are questions posed repeatedly to local Community Health Councils which demonstrate the need for public education on matters related to the use and provision of health services. Additionally there are repeated demands on professional workers, from parents-to-be, young parents or people reaching retirement indicating a need for subject-based, verbal and written educative materials.

Data can be found through individual practitioners, groups of professionals discovering a common factor of need, statistical returns or other public documents, and personal records of clients or patients. To make a successful assessment the assessor will, to the best of his or her ability, check the accuracy and validity of the data. It has to be made quite clear whether an assessment is based on fact or assumption. The latter may be sound professional judgement, but has to be clearly justified and understandable to others.

Assessment of need

Assessment of need, based on data and professional judgement, will divide logically into several parts.

First, it must be established whether or not this is a new need. If it is new, the plan of action may lead to new and hopefully imaginative approaches. If it is a need rooted in the past, previous measures will have to be considered. There may have been no attempt to alleviate the situation, and the assessor should know the reasons for this, or there may have been any number of attempts with limited or no success. The different methods which had been tried will have to be assessed in turn, so that lessons can be learnt and utilized from success or lack of it.

Second, it is important to gauge the acceptability of the need; is it recognized by professional workers only, or accepted as important by the proposed recipient of any action?

Third, the immediacy and urgency of needs has to be given a priority rating, and decisions reached as to those which require short-, medium- or long-term strategies incorporated in planning and actions.

Fourth, the type and nature of the need for which the process is being implemented has to be established. The variations on this theme could be endless. A few concrete examples follow.

Individual needs

1. Young persons adjusting to leaving school and entering the world of work or unemployment.
2. Persons of any age coping with new life-styles, or increasing disability.
3. Young parents wishing to provide more adequately for their families.
4. Persons of any age coping with loss or bereavement.
5. Learning about illness or disability of a family member and the available care provision including self-help.

Group needs

1. Preparation for parenthood.
2. Safety at work or play.
3. Increased knowledge of human development, and bodily maintenance.
4. Successful interpersonal relationships.
5. Alleviation of loneliness and isolation, e.g., in a new housing estate.

Community needs

1. Promotion of a healthier attitude to life and living.
2. Prevention of health breakdown, infectious diseases or infestations.
3. Adjustments to changes, such as massive unemployment.
4. Utilization of increased leisure time.
5. Appropriate use of health services, knowledge of their availability and range.

National needs

1. Interpretation of policies and their effects.
2. Linking a national campaign with local efforts.
3. Introducing new, research-based knowledge and its applications.

International needs

1. Active participation in planning of primary health care.

2. Active participation in meetings and congresses.

3. Supplying evidence of successes of schemes of health education.

Fifth, consideration of needs of the provider of services or health education. This is a much neglected aspect of all professional work, but the motivation, state of knowledge, ability and possibility of job satisfaction could influence to a great extent the success or otherwise of any plan and action.

Assessment of available resources, including people and time, is vital; it is very easy to assume that resources are meagre, people with expertise being the scarcest of all resources, and that time is at a premium. The assessor should take account of readily available resources, those which might be obtained, and those which have not been considered previously. Many professionals undertaking assessments of this kind forget peripheral resources, which might usefully be tapped, such as local industry and commerce, and the interest of voluntary groups. The widest possible scan should be made, often the most surprising discoveries emerge as a result.

Analysis of assessment and plan of action

Thorough assessment leads naturally to a plan of action. The analysis of assessments links the two phases and provides a base-line. Analysis of data should show the scale of any required action, indicate parameters, resources, time-scale, manpower needs and draw attention to further needs which may become obvious through implementation. The first step in the planning phase is to clarify the parameters for action, and establish priorities if this is necessary. Any definition of parameters must include the state of knowledge current at the time in the locality for which the plan is being evolved, superstitions and beliefs. It must enable practitioners to build upon these varied and sometimes rocky foundations, and allow sufficient flexibility for adaptation and progress.

The second step in the planning phase is the formulation of objectives. The agreed objectives should be acceptable to all involved in the proposed action, and may need to be communicated before the plan can be put into practice.

Assessment and its analysis should point the way forward to new approaches to situations, the plan of action should define and refine the methods and means to be used. One recipe for success could be to agree to forget established practice and use current trends and technology as the means. One very successful health-education activity recently used pop-music as its vehicle. When planning to overcome intransient problems, the pitfalls unearthed by previous attempts should be avoided, and the elements which led to successes strengthened. Where assessment has shown that the recipient is unlikely to view the perceived need in the same way as professionals, a sales technique will be an essential part of the plan, creating awareness of the situation before offering one or more ways towards solution.

Phasing must be inherent in any plan, allowing for short- and long-term effects. The phases must be clearly defined, or it would be possible, if not probable, that no sustained effort or effect will be achieved. In any event, plans should include reinforcement of knowledge and reaffirmation of newly aquired attitudes at specified intervals, based on the fact that human memory is fallible, and permanent change of attitude or behaviour can only be realized when new ideas and behaviour have become habitual.

Assessment will have described the types of need to be met, active planning must pay close attention to the variables involved and accommodate as many as possible. Built-in flexibility is a useful element of any plan; it is essential in health education which aims to give people more freedom of choice based on increased knowledge, and has to acknowledge the recipients' right to accept, reject or modify any information given by professionals. A plan draughted in partnership with prospective receipients stands the best chance of success.

A plan which does not incorporate the needs of the provider is likely to go awry. It should therefore include up-dating of knowledge of the health educator, and, if possible, a professional support network for reinforcement, analysis of motivation and attitudes which may encourage and enable, or hinder, achievements.

Plans often do not come to fruition, or are less than successful in practice, because insufficient detail has been included about resources. Goodwill is a sound start, but all aspects should be considered. This may lead to a way of organizing existing widely spread possibilities, and demonstrate the benefits of providing those resources which are not available at that time or place. Whilst there may be an urge to meet needs as quickly as possible, i.e., to be seen to do something, this can often hinder success in the long term. Sound foundations, based on effective assessment and planning are the surest recipe for success.

People constitute the most important resource and it is necessary to establish their strengths, e.g. expertise, personal appeal or charisma, or an innate aptitude and ability for health teaching. Where several people are likely to be involved in the execution of a planned programme, whether this is a mixture of professionals or of professionals and volunteers, the role of the co-ordinator will have to be defined and agreed. Contributions to action will vary in quantity and quality and the plan must encompass this variability. Proposed recipients of health education form a resource in themselves, and their contribution may need to be structured or guided.

The nature of communications to be used, their appropriateness and clarity, the avoidance or use of jargon, and commonality of language or possible language barriers are important elements of any plan.

The person taking the role of health educator may be regarded by the recipients as an example for good or ill. Planning should utilize personal potential to its fullest measure.

Physical facilities, as part of resources, are considered by many people to be a vital element. This may be true of formal or academic teaching and learning, but health education should be able to 'cash in' on existing bases, irrespective of whether these are ample or the opposite. Some of the most underused existing bases for health education are waiting rooms in surgeries, clinics and hospitals, in direct contrast to waiting rooms at most dentists and vets, where waiting periods usually prove useful and informative. The reasons for this lack of use are manifold, but a well-laid plan could overcome these. To utilize certain sites or bases the planner will have to ascertain their availability and accessibility; train and bus strikes can play havoc with the best-laid plans. The physical comfort and ease of potential learners may or may not play an important part in implementation of any plan, but certainly an easy manner of approach on the part of professionals and a friendly welcome will help greatly.

The nature and length of sessions, additional requirements such as teaching aids, tea or coffee, facilities for accompanying adults or children, heating and lighting, direction signs and other details form the bread and butter of planning. Knowledge of basic facts about the planned programme by all involved is also important, including the likely age range of a group, the expected number of participants, whether the audience is composed of voluntary attenders, or whether participation has been enforced by external pressures. Preoccupations which could affect active participation and be a barrier to learning could all affect the plan of action.

Finally, teaching methods have to be decided and planned. Any method of teaching and learning, or any combination of methods may be agreed upon. All the above points contribute to the choice of methods, and personal preference and expertise of the educator may be decisive. Planning for success is the most time-consuming phase of the process, but it pays dividends in outcomes, especially in the long term. It becomes easier with practice, as repeated planning is likely to include the same range of factors. This familiarity is likely to lead to another positive result, in that it allows measures of progress and achievement to be made.

Action according to plan

One part of the planning phase was the formulation of objectives. The first action may well be to accept or modify these statements, and make them more specific to practice. Health education, being rooted in practice and reality, needs an essentially practical approach. Objectives reiterated as part of action may form part of an implicit contract between provider and recipient to achieve the desired outcomes.

Teaching by objectives, either in behavioural terms or descriptive fashion, is a favourite tool of some educationalists. The Open University has gone furthest, or, at least, was the first public body to state detailed objectives for each part of a teaching programme. Most successful plans are descriptive, not proscriptive or prescriptive, and another action may be to confirm the decisions reached by planning. In all other ways action should be a logical, sequential implementation of the plan — teaching or educating, furthering discussions of relevant issues and using the resources, methods and time-scale laid down in the agreed plan.

The final action should be to note and communicate any part of the plan which has not been completely followed by action, and will, therefore, require subsequent action or follow-up. The reasons for incompleteness, any new ideas and items arising out of the implementation can also be the cornerstones for the next phases of evaluation and modification.

Those health educators with nursing background or orientation will feel most satisfied at this phase of the health-education process, which is the 'doing' phase, but it must be remembered that satisfaction can only be maintained with continued achievement, and that the latter requires all phases to be successfully completed. The satisfaction of recipients is of equal importance to the feelings of practitioners.

Evaluation

Evaluation of health education is very important, as it provides the yardstick for future actions and developments. It is also one objective of

WHO, and is seen as providing the means of increased success and achievement throughout member countries.

The meaning of evaluation is not always clear. In its strictest sense it means a researched analysis of all available data, an assessment of value or worth. The value accorded to any given item or activity will vary depending on the interests or biases of the evaluator. Managers are likely to look for cost-effectiveness of actions, and for full utilization of skills and resources; professionals are likely to see evaluation in terms of goal achievement; recipients may be unable to make any comment on value until long after the event, when it has proven useful, or otherwise, in their daily life.

Tools for evaluation of health-education activities have not yet been perfected, though a number of people are attempting to find ways of using other processes of evaluation in a suitable format. At present evaluators of this process have to use whatever means are to hand, and through this exercise may establish which tool is the most useful for effective evaluation. Although this phase of the process is not perfect, one of the things it should not be is a mechanism for criticizing. The term evaluation is seen as threatening by many professionals as it implies a value judgement of their activities, and, occasionally, does contain adverse comments. It should, however, become a positive stage towards progress and any criticism it contains should be constructive and helpful.

This phase of the health-education process is intended to be a positive move towards enhancements of future activities, leading to the achievement of the broad objectives of Health for All, and should enable improvements in practice of teaching, planning, management or provision of care.

There are several pointers to successful evaluation:

Immediate reactions, of both teacher and taught, provide feedback, which contributes to the whole. Immediate reactions may be coloured by the tenor of the experience, and consideration of results may be more objective if it takes place a reasonable time after the event—not so long that it has become forgotten or overlaid, and not so short that there has been no opportunity for recovery of equilibrium. Some health-education activities require a longitudinal, long-term, repeated evaluation to show the results stated in the objectives.

Ideally, evaluation should be based on measurements, which are universally acceptable and recognizable. It appears to be self-defeating to attempt to obtain an absolute measurement for the results of health teaching, as one of its aims is likely to be a continuing one, based on human progress and development. It is, however, possible to obtain broad measurements in terms of response, demands arising out of the activity, needs met and new needs discovered, as well as some evidence of changed behaviour or attitudes. David Cohen in 'Prevention as an Economic Good' (1981) sees the essential question in health-education evaluation as being whether behaviour will be altered as a result, or whether health status is affected, not just whether information was received and understood or attitudes modifed.

Changes in behaviour may not be immediately apparent, nor will it be evident whether such changes are temporary or permanent, but they should manifest in future patterns of epidemiology. Research to date has only been able to measure short-term results, as shown in questionnaire or examination results. Feedback from any type of activity can be obtained on at least three levels. First, from the recipient, by words or actions; second, from the provider, preferably in report form; and, third, from interested third parties who may have a vested interest or who may be able to act as objective assessors. Feedback is therefore one useful tool for evaluation.

There is considerable debate regarding the objectivity of any evaluation. In such a wide field as health education, both objective and subjective judgements can be valuable. The two should be clearly differentiated, and the rationale for the latter provided.

The evaluation phase of the process must include consideration of the match or mismatch of information given and received. In many instances professionals have been unaware that their words and actions have been misunderstood or given very different interpretations.

Evaluation is part of professional accountability to self, clients or patients, managers and employers and to the general public as a whole, whose tax and insurance contributions pay the wages of most health educators. Employers have a responsibility to see that resources, especially money, are used wisely and that time and effort are not wasted, and employees may be required to provide proof of success.

Modification and reassessment

Professional roles and functions do not cease with the completion of one activity, but require the routine application of valuable techniques. The health-education process could become one such technique, but it has a fifth phase on which continuing activity and routine application should be based.

Successful evaluation should guide towards appropriate modifications of subsequent actions. It should highlight any factor omitted from the initial assessment, and show positive and negative outcomes which should determine the bias of future activity. There may have been aspects of planning which did not prove feasible, and which, therefore, require modification, or it may not have been possible to complete the plan of action. Modification and reassessment will lead to realignment of planning.

During this phase it may be possible to determine what reinforcement of teaching is required for maximum effect, and indicate areas which would benefit by formal research before teaching can be as effective as the goals would indicate. Modification may be possible in view of changed circumstances or facilities, and reassessment will ensure that changes are communicated to all those involved. Reassessment may lead to amended facilities for practitioners, such as enhancement of teaching skills, or utilization of different resources.

A value judgement of the process

The process approach, if used as a tool for improved practice, has unquestioned beneficial value. The hazard of the process becoming an end in itself can be avoided. There is a distinct need, particularly at a time of economic stringency, scarce resources and a challenge to professional practice, to carry out professional practice to the best of one's ability, and to be seen to be doing so. The process should lead to both these, as well as resulting in better services for the public. A process approach also leads to a continuous review of practice, which is essential if it is to remain valid, relevant, up-to-date and effective. The process, as described, may at first seem cumbersome, time consuming and even a nuisance. However, it is just an extension of what many practitioners have been doing implicitly, without formalizing or documenting their methods.

It is helpful to document the first, second, fourth and fifth phases of the process, however briefly. This provides evidence and tools for self-audit, future actions, and reasoned arguments to be used in so many ways and situations. Accountability is becoming a major issue, especially in terms of use and allocation of resources, including trained staff. Using the process is one way of demonstrating professional accountability and effectiveness.

Each time a process approach is used, the time and effort required become less, until it becomes habitual, though not a habit which cannot be refined and improved. The use of the process clearly demonstrates skills inherent in health education, either as a contributor or as the main function within one's work.

Further reading

Barton, L and Tomlinson, S (1981) Special Education: Policy, Practices and Social Issues, Harper & Row.

Cohen, D (1981) Prevention as an Economic Good, Health Economics Research Unit, Discussion Paper 02/81, University of Aberdeen

Hendy, A (1982) The nursing process in health visiting, address at the 1982 HVA conference (to be published in The Health Visitor)

Marriner, A (1975) The Nursing Process, C V Mosby

Maslow, A (1954) Motivation and Personality, Harper & Row

Illich, I et al. (1977) Disabling Professions, Open Forum Series, Marion Boyars

Redman, B K (1980) The Process of Patient Teaching in Nursing, C V Mosby

Sutherland, I (1979) Health Education, George Allen & Unwin

Wainwright, P (1982) Health education and the nursing process, Nurse Education Today 2(2):16

CHAPTER 7

METHODS OF HEALTH EDUCATION

Triumph of Goodness, Order, Discipline and Education over the forces of evil, violence, ignorance and destruction.

Chapel of St Benedict (of Nursia), Peterborough Cathedral

Methodology is the bread and butter of health education, the tools used in daily practice. Any good craftsman has his favourite set of tools which have been tried and tested and are kept in good working order. He also experiments with adaptations of his tools for specific purposes and develops new patents. Usually he is a little reluctant to move towards very new equipment, but will try any new machinery or development to see whether it can help to further his skills and lead to greater achievements. Most developments come about through contact with craftsmen of a similar frame of mind, and mutual encouragement and exchange of information.

Health educators are skilled craftspeople, educational methods are their tools, and they have a need to develop and adapt the methods to meet a great variety of situations and changing environments and needs. The methods they can use at any time are dependent on the situation in which they work, the facilities available and the client groups with whom they deal. Clients have come to expect, through exposure to mass media and greater knowledge levels, expertise in teaching methods. They, like the teachers, are initially suspicious of strange and new ways, but very often welcome experiments, especially if they know they are part and partner to such trials.

Health educators have tried most traditional methods of teaching and are developing some new ones. There does not appear to be any one method which covers all situations, or which proves so much better than the rest that its use should become exclusive. The most successful ways are to consider which method is appropriate for each situation or session, allow flexibility, and be prepared to try something else if the first does not provide expected results. Any tool or method requires practice in its use. Any practitioner can develop and enhance his skills in using tools, through repeated effort and constant application.

Lectures

The most traditional teaching method is the lecture, address or talk. Some lectures can be interesting, but they require the recipients to be sponges, soaking up information, and the ability and facility to sit in one place for sufficiently long to absorb the information. Their impact is only valuable if it provides additional, not basic, information and builds on existing expertise or knowledge. Few people, especially the client groups encountered in health education, want to be sponges, and few health-care facilities provide the environment which is conducive to concentrated listening. So the use of lectures is limited in the context of health education, with the exception, perhaps, of educating the educator.

Participation

The value of participation is evident in many ways. Any method which involves learners and stimulates them to take an active part is likely to result in a greater degree of internalization, continuation of learning processes and new thoughts about the matters in which participation has taken place. Participation often brings its own reinforcements of learning as the participants may relate their contribution to third parties, providing their own revision of the material. People vary in their willingness and ability to participate, from total involvement to occasional, hesitant contributions. The latter usually increase with familiarity.

Most methods available to the health educator are participatory. A few which are more formal, can be adapted to lead to participation in a limited or subsequent way. Participation is relevant for all age and target groups, young people are likely to be more familiar with this way of learning. Older people often do not associate it with learning, but are familiar with talking about their experiences. This basis can be used to build the participative process and create involvement.

Participation cannot be one-sided, teacher and learners should each play their part. Many professionals do not find this easy, as it means reconsidering their position and role, and avoiding dominance, obvious, directive leadership or overt control. There is an element of fear in participation, as one gives of self, and some people use professionalism as a cloak or protection which they do not wish to breach. On the positive side, by participating, professionals extend their skills, knowledge and experience, and may find the development inherent in participative methods of teaching a welcome challenge.

Control can be one aspect of professional practice, control not in a traditional or authoritarian sense, but in ensuring that all members of the group are treated fairly, that everyone is given the opportunity to participate and that materials are not misused. Guidance, rather than dominance, is exercised as the teacher is the expert on the subject and may wish to inject specific information, ensure that the agreed programme is more or less followed and that personal or harmful discussion is curtailed if necessary. The health educator may carry responsibility for the outcomes of any session and therefore require to establish a balance between full participation and formal input.

Discussion

Most health education is based on discussion of a topic or a range of topics. Usually this means that the health educator introduces the matter for discussion, and then allows participation, acting as leader to the discussion and keeping it topic related. In this instance the role of the teacher is to ensure that everyone who wishes to contribute does so, and that all the threads of the discussion are drawn together and summarized at the end. Many people find this the most comfortable and successful method of teaching.

There are variations in organizing discussion, which may be helpful for some people and groups. First, the discussion could be structured so that component parts of the topic receive input and consideration in a logical sequence or a sequence relevant to the participants. This ensures coverage of any agenda or programme and can lead from the particular to broad concepts or vice versa. Generally, the results of the discussion are summarized verbally by the health educator. It may be of long-term benefit if the summary were written or recorded, so that it can be utilized by others. The benefits are for both teachers and learners; the teacher for planning and evaluating other sessions, the learner for reinforcement and reference. The summary could usefully be made by one of the members of the group, which would serve additional purposes, such as ensuring that there is no misunderstanding and that all points of interest to the group have been considered. It could also indicate the priorities important to the target group and help with on-going health education.

Second, discussions could be free and easy, taking account of the interest paramount within the group, and only limited by health content or related topics. This can be useful in an ad hoc way, but requires great skill on the part of the teacher and may make excessive demands on expertise. It presupposes that the teacher's knowledge base is wide, and adequate information and references are at hand. Free discussion should also be summarized, verbally, in writing or on tape, which would lead naturally to clarification of those aspects which may merit further attention.

Third, discussion can be subsequent to the use of other methods of teaching, such as films. Sufficient time must be available and allowance made for diversity of opinions to be expressed.

The physical climate in which discussion takes place plays a vital part in its content and effect. A noisy draughty room, uncomfortable chairs, inability to hear what people are saying or being unable to see the other speakers all mitigate against successful outcomes. Luxury is not required, but reasonable conditions are.

Demonstration

At one time every programme of teaching used to include demonstrations of some sort or another, for example bathing a baby or making a feed. There is, however, merit in showing practical aspects, whilst recognizing that for some things there may be no one correct way of proceeding. The teacher does not have to be the demonstrator, some of the target group members may be at least as expert, and the group will enjoy the success of one of their own. One must be realistic; it is no use demonstrating perfection, when people present live in imperfect conditions. Demonstrations, and subsequent practice at the skill, can be fun and lead to discussion of matters related to the skill demonstrated. Demonstrations can also be nervewracking, as they show up any lack of expertise, and are prone to mischances.

Role play

Every professional health educator has heard of role play, and groans or beams at the word, according to their own experience. It is a useful method of teaching and learning, and can be developed as a useful tool. It is only one method, however, not THE method.

The origins of role play are simple. Children at play do it automatically, unselfconsciously and learn life-skills from it. Few children have not played, or been encouraged to play, mothers and fathers, hospitals, schools and all the other exciting roles they see about them. As people get older and socialized into a professional role, they become more self-conscious. They are, therefore, naturally reluctant to expose these actions to public scrutiny through role play. However, role play can show the possible range of actions in any given situation, and help practitioners to choose their future actions and behaviour in a constructive manner.

Role play in health education has a similar purpose; people who have difficulty in expressing their thoughts, are enabled through role play to act the part — of angry mother, of worried father, of objectionable neighbour, of unacceptable professional, etc. This can be helpful in expressing concerns, in clarifying their stance and in self-realization of the full meaning of the role. It can also lead to consideration of the role from a range of perspectives and adjustment of it. Role play can be fun, even if indulged in by adults, and can allow them to relax in being someone else.

Variations on role play are the use of dolls or puppets. In some instances, if the role is played by a puppet, the person holding the puppet will perform in an identical way to that described above, except that they express themselves through the puppet. In other instances puppets can be used to portray a range of characters outside the experience of the group. Dolls and puppets do not have to be beautifully made, a glove and some paint or make-up will do. Groups may enjoy making a puppet representing their most loved or hated figure, which can also be a useful tool for health education.

In some instances role play has been enhanced for elements of professional education by introducing actors among the learners. The actors hold a specific brief which requires the professional to respond appropriately. In this way strengths and weaknesses of practice are discovered and can be rectified. This means could be transposed to health education, as could the performance of short plays, poems or variety acts. Drama and theatrical performance in health education have not yet been fully explored or developed.

Projects

Projects are often used in health education in schools, when children discover as much as they can about a given topic before discussing it and drawing conclusions for the whole group. The discovery method of learning is considered successful by professional educators, teachers, and has proved itself in subject-based health education.

Projects have rarely been used in health education of adults but they may be a useful method. Projects do not have to be long or consist of written material. A target group may be persuaded to record a critique of the health services available in their area, to make a video-film of encouraging and stimulating their children towards constructive play, or to draw their impressions of health-service personnel. Each would be a two-way educative tool, revealing to the educator, showing up shortfalls, and demonstrating the ability of the group to each other. The means of carrying out such projects are becoming available in many health authorities; authorities may have the equipment somewhere within their stocks, and it is often underused.

Games

Games are one of the most effective and underutilized methods in health education. They are often considered childish, and therefore inappropriate, or remain unrecognized for the messages they could contain. There has been some research into the use of games, and results indicate that they could usefully be more widely used.

Success is likely to be enhanced as many people enjoy a gamble and are familiar with the principles of gaming. They also like the competitive element, and are likely to make great efforts to 'win'. They usually retain a high percentage of information, with a view to future competitiveness, but also use the information to consider the appropriate health behaviour for them. Games are a popular medium for all ages, and leads to their use within families and the community, i.e., outside the health-education structure, but of benefit to future health-education activities.

Card games

Card games are a popular pastime. They have elements of fun, competition, skill and knowledge and can be used by small or large groups. Cards could illustrate almost any life situation, but they may take some time to develop, print and test for application. Their use is spreading, health educators may need to persuade commercial companies to assist in their development. Two examples of card games are the Open University's pack designed for professional education relating to nonaccidental injury (this pack can usefully be used in the subject area with any group) and the French Health

Education Committee's attractive pack 'Jeu mangez juste', which can be played like canasta and includes information on principles of nutrition, food values, recipies and suggested menus.

Puzzles

Puzzles are popular with young and old alike. There are a few crossword puzzles and other competitive teasers which appear in the press and may mark anniversaries of famous people, such as scientists and inventors of modern treatments. Of the vast numbers of jigsaw puzzles produced commercially, there do not appear to be any which depict items related to good health. A few commercial firms wishing to advertise health products have produced puzzles for children, but the scale and scope has been small. Each school child in France is presented with a jigsaw puzzle, which builds up the body of Action Man, as it should be if looked after properly. The whole usage of puzzles has not been sufficiently explored or developed in the context of health education, but it could represent a fertile medium and method.

Educative toys

Educative toys are popular with parents and children, and they deal with almost all aspects of education, except health. There is no reason why they could not be extended in their usage. Puppets and their value have already been mentioned, and their use could become more wide-spread.

Competitions

Competitions are worthy of consideration. There is an element of competition in the activities of groups using sports as a medium for health, but this could also be extended for the purpose of health education.

Video and computer games

Video and computer games are a rapidly growing way to enjoy leisure time. They appeal to young and old, and are almost addictive for some. Health educators should advise manufacturers of games which could contain health messages, and urge that those used in public places include some with a positive health education element. It may be a pleasure to think of someone addicted to health, but the games could incorporate a time switch, which prevents their use for unlimited lengths of time. The range of these games is increasing and they should become a vehicle for health education.

Games people play

'Getting to know you and all about you' games have increasingly been used in professional education. They should make a valuable contribution, but there is, as yet, insufficient skill in their usage among health educators. Johari windows, i.e., seeing yourself as others see you, dyadic encounters, sculpting of family and problem situations, and name associations are a few of the common techniques using gaming as a base. However, they should be used with care. They are particularly useful when the subject is the development of personal relationships.

The games people play have become well recognized since Berne's writings, and it is clear that we are all involved in gaming and playing every day of our lives. We play the part of mother, father, nurse, adviser, comforter, teacher and so on. The game factor can be channelled to type-cast some people, and the danger is, of course, stereotyping. The result is that some people gain confidence and competence through acting a role, and that life gives everybody a diversity of roles. The game factor can be utilized in health education, and achieve a move forward in attitude and behaviour modification.

Experiential learning

Experiential learning is the in-phrase for much participatory activity. It really means using a relaxed atmosphere and sufficient time, giving the opportunity to learn in the style and manner most acceptable to the individual, and most beneficial in the long term through a combination of all the above methods. Some people are refining methods of participation and learning activities, and may prove that there is a method which is superior to the rest. This stage has not yet been reached. Experiential learning implies full participation, and it may be unrealistic to expect everybody to expose themselves to this, however desirable the outcome. It also implies a lowering of the defence mechanisms which everybody builds for himself against outsiders, and time is crucial to provide a replacement for this important coping facility.

Visual teaching materials

Films

Films permeate today's society, and they have been used in health education for some time. They can be useful, but need to be carefully selected. Many films are clearer on second viewing. People have come to expect a high standard of technical production and projection, and many health educators are unable to meet these criteria through lack of resources. Most authorities have a stock of films which are easily available and there are several film libraries which include materials useful for health education. Whilst films may be an attractive method of teaching, it can be costly, both to obtain the most up-to-date material and the equipment which will do it justice, and the teacher has to be able to preview the film in order to extract relevant points and answer any questions. Films are considered to have a life of no more than 5 years, after which they lose currency — those stored by many authorities are older than this. Some commercial companies have made excellent films on specific subjects, but, again, preview and careful use are essential. Video recorders are becoming more generally available and these could replace the hiring and use of films, allowing the sort of editing which would particularize the film to specific usage and provide involvement of the target group. It is estimated that home video recorders will become commonplace within the next few years, so health educators should now become expert in their use. The great advantage of video recordings is that they can be stopped and started at will, allowing discussion of component parts, return and review. The current, but decreasing, disadvantage is that film-tape and recorder must match, and are not interchangeable. Conditions of copyright must also be observed, but can usually be overcome especially if any recorded tape is used for one specific purpose only, and not retained for repeated use.

Trigger films

Trigger films are a useful tool to present an issue and start a debate. They can be used for almost any health-education subject, and are usually short and relevant. Some have been available in educational film libraries for many years, others are being developed by such agents as the Health Education Council. There is little to prevent health educators making their own short films, utilizing the facilities available at their local college of further or higher education.

Slide/tape programmes

Slide/tape programmes are mainly available from the medical services library. They are useful in a limited way, and need careful handling as not all the material may be suitable for the planned session or the time available.

Slides selected specially for the purpose of the teaching session are often more useful.

Radio and television

Radio and television are discussed in the chapter on mass media (Chapter 10), but for this purpose television can be a useful medium for health education. Video-taping can enhance the value as programmes can be used in the context of planned sessions. Health educators could use the media in the nature of homework, by drawing attention to relevant programmes and basing discussion on the viewing or listening which has taken place outside the ambit of the educator. Many participants will have watched different programmes, and therefore they form part of incidental methods of teaching.

Advertising

Advertising is often criticized for its harmful effects. It can be incorporated in visual materials used for health education, in part to counterbalance any harmful effects and in part to build upon and use as another means of triggering discussion.

Written materials

The clientele of the health educator will include those who read voraciously and those who read hardly at all — even those who are unable to read. Any written material has, therefore, to be carefully selected.

Posters

Posters use the minimum of writing to maximum effect. A plethora of posters is made available to health educators by commercial concerns and some are available from the Health Education Council and similar sources with specific health messages. They can create an attractive backcloth to other health-education activities, be a source of questions and elaboration, and act as triggers to discussion. They are often underused, because they are left too long in one place, or juxtaposed to material which detracts from their impact. The maximum life of a poster in one place before it starts to suffer from overexposure is 1 month to 6 weeks. The time for homemade posters is generally past, in view of the range of such material which is presently available. However, somebody who is especially adept at producing such materials could make a useful contribution, and some posters may need adaptation for local conditions. Writing on posters should be large, colourful and clear. Graphical representation of the message is helpful. If a poster is made for a specific purpose, it occasionally helps to draw attention through deliberate mistakes.

Leaflets, pamphlets and books

Leaflets, pamphlets and books of various sizes abound. Their usefulness and relevance is as variable as the material itself. As a method of teaching they have distinct limitations, as a means of enhancement of learning, of follow-up and reiteration they can be of maximum use. It is unwise to recommend material which has not been scrutinized, as this is bound to crop up in later sessions or discussion.

Handouts

Handouts to supplement a session are infrequently used in health education, though they are common practice in education. They are a useful adjunct, as they can carry the discussion beyond the site of the session, and provide continuity of information flow. Handouts should be relevant, short, clear and precise, giving figures and references where appropriate.

Minutes and reports

Minutes or reports are commonly used in many areas, but not in health education. It has been suggested above that a written summary of discussion might prove valuable, reports can also have their uses. Many people welcome being able to show what they have been doing, and such a written supplement would help. It may increase the immediate work involved in providing health education, but could shorten it in the long term, and certainly make it more appropriate, by avoiding repetition.

The health educator as an exemplar

Although this point has been left as the last in the chapter, it is not the least important. Voluntarily or involuntarily the health educator is likely to be seen as an example by the target group. This raises a number of issues, as it does mean that it is impossible to draw a dividing line between private, personal and professional life. It is important to be aware that the health educator is regarded in this way, and make personal and professional decisions with the full knowledge of this.

The fact of being an example does not imply that the health educator has to be perfect, human qualities and failings are as much appreciated by target groups as perfection. It does mean that there has to be self-awareness, and sometimes open admission of failings and feelings. Clients are very conscious of the image presented to them, and may compare it with the image they have of the person through other channels. Mismatch can hamper communications.

It is a moot point whether health educators should alter their own life-styles to be able to present a desirable image, or whether they accept the image they do portray. Clothing, make-up, the way a uniform is worn, posture, habits, mannerisms all come into the formation of the image. Many health educators are able to counteract any physical image they may present, by their approach, manner or professional stance. The fact of being an example is not detrimental to health education, it has to be recognized and accepted.

Being seen as an examplar can create personal and professional conflict, which can only be resolved on an individual basis. The conflict created in this way should not reach harmful proportions, but may require the use of professional networks and peer-support to resolve. Most professionals accept some group norms, they in turn influence and confirm the norms of their peer group. If an individual decides to deviate from explicit or implicit group norms, they should do this as part of a conscious decision. The peer-support thus gained can help in reinforcing, or otherwise, the images presented to or received by learners and client groups.

Further reading

Beard, R and Bligh, D (1971) Research into Teaching Methods, Society for Research into Higher Education Ltd

Berne, E (1975) What Do You Say After You Say Hello?, Corgi

Brandes, D and Phillips, H (1979) Gamesters Handbook, Hutchinson

Pfeiffer, J and Jones, J (1974) Handbook of Structured Experiences in Human Relationship Training, University Associates US

Other sources

Film libraries catalogues

Health Education Index

Health education booklets produced by local health-education departments

CHAPTER 8

TARGET GROUPS IN HEALTH EDUCATION

We never will have all we need. Expectation will always exceed demand.

Aneurin Bevan (1948)

Target groups have, until now, been an inherent part of the provision of health education by health workers and official agencies. These groups have been selected according to policies and pressures of governments or politicians, biases of ministers of health, stated policies and priorities of employing authorities, expressed demands and pressures applied by special interest groups within any community and the interests or perceived needs of health educators. Provision for any group has been constrained by available resources, premises, staff and time. Objectives for health education have been limited, though they may have formed part of a broad and more general pattern. Provision for any one group, by its very existence, limits the availability of services for other groups whose needs and rights may be fundamentally the same, but whose expectations are disappointed or who are not as obvious and vocal in making their demands and views known. Each health educator, therefore, has to ask himself whether he is providing his services and expertise for the greatest number of possible clients, whether he should be reaching other groups and, if he has to formulate priorities because of constraints and limitations, how these priorities are determined (Figure 4).

The World Health Organization has made 'Health for all by the year 2000' the overall aim for the provision of health care and health education. A major international conference on primary health care, held at Alma-Ata in 1978, reaffirmed this principle. The conference resulted in a public statement which has become known as the Alma-Ata declaration. A copy of the statement is given in Appendix II. All member states of WHO have agreed to work towards this common goal. Each country will need to devise

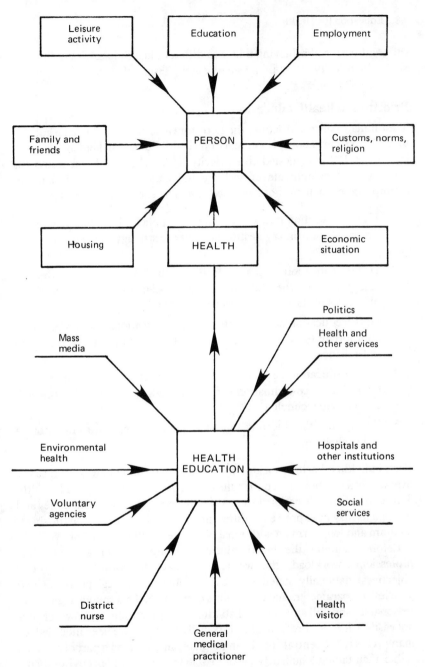

Figure 4 A model of health care and health education

different means of achieving this, and different health hazards are likely to shape the priority rating in the staging and phasing of efforts.

Priorities in health education

To stimulate concerted action, the Director General of WHO, in an address to the XIth International Conference on Health Education held in Tasmania in August 1982, suggested five priority approaches, and elaborated the urgency of developments of seeking and using new methods and for attempting to reach *all*, not a selected few. The stated priorities are:

1. Health education needs to develop new policies in harmony with the principles of primary health care and the strategy of health for all by the year 2000.

2. Health education needs to facilitate the development of human resources with the skill to translate social goals into educational objectives for health for all by the year 2000.

3. Health education needs to reflect on the educational technology most appropriate to promote individual and community involvement and self-reliance.

4. Health education needs to strengthen its multisectoral approach and to increase co-ordination of health education efforts through appropriate technology.

5. Finally, health education must pay greater attention to monitoring and evaluation.

Each individual health educator will have to determine how to fit into the overall pattern, how to contribute to the targets set for world health. Through individuals national and local policies are shaped, though they and their plans may be expressed in different ways, and concentrate in the short, medium and long term on additional objectives to those stated above.

Before planning the health-education component of an individual professional workload, the worker will have to consider the WHO objectives, nationally stated policies and objectives, local pressures and policies and parameters and constraints of practice. This sounds logical and reasonable, and will already be a habit for some practitioners; however, it is not easily achieved. Professionals, especially nurses, have been moulded for many years to concentrate on the immediate, and often on a part of a person rather than taking a holistic view of people in their complex environments and relationships. It is also easier to define a target group, such as expectant parents, than to consider this group as part of the whole community. Pregnancy and parenthood are one small part of the life cycle. They represent a phase with special and definable needs, but they do not occur in isolation and arise naturally from other phases of life, as well as leading naturally to involvement in many aspects of community life, such as shopping and leisure activities, schooling and employment, using many of the health, education and social services, being a rent and rate payer and eligible to vote in local and national elections. Each involvement encompasses a range of personal and public relationships, and one important objective for health education should be to enable relationships to be formed and developed, to consider the whole range of human interactions and encourage more positive human contacts. Health educators could be central to this important aspect of life, by acting as enablers, catalysts and encouragers.

Monitoring and evaluating such broad activities is difficult. It is simpler to set simple targets, and measure outcomes in small doses. The pattern of community activity, morbidity and breakdown in human relationships and interactions will supply the tools for monitoring and provide a guide to achievements or lack of them.

It is often said that we live in a violent society, and evidence of violence or aggression can be found everywhere, in every newspaper and most news-broadcasts, to the exclusion of positive and more pleasant matters. The root causes of violence have never been proven, though many have been suggested. Health education might assist in making society less overtly aggressive through

1. Teaching improved interpersonal relationships.
2. Diffusing potential violence.
3. Suggesting more beneficial outlets for inbuilt tensions.
4. Creating greater awareness of human potential.
5. Demonstrating the healthy need for anger.
6. Utilizing anger to achieve something positive and tangible.

It is tempting to say that it is more comfortable to aim at small achievements, with known target groups, limited objectives and measurable outcomes, and hope that someone else will co-ordinate efforts, and that each little bit will contribute to the grand total. The year 2000 is soon, a very short space of time in which to achieve a tremendous amount.

Every contribution is likely to add to the total effort and effect, but no professional can any longer afford to consider their contribution in isolation from the rest, nor refuse the challenge of aiming for the broad target with every opportunity that presents itself. Every lack of contribution will detract from the total effort and possible achievement.

One professional responsibility of health educators should be to move towards incorporating the broad goals into their individual targets, and making conscious efforts towards the overall aim with each group and within each plan of action. This may entail a process of education of one professional by another, it certainly necessitates interprofessional communications at their best, and may also require a redefinition of targets set by local managements or national policies. The latter may sound impossibly remote, but as each nation has agreed to the stated overall objective, national and local policies and priorities must eventually reflect the agreement. Health educators should act as aide-memoires and enable acceleration of concerted efforts. To do this, they will have to find the means to overcome inertia, apathy, poor communication networks, and, in some instances, hierarchical and authoritarian strategies and relationships. There is no easy way, but acceleration of current achievements and efforts will create its own increasing impetus.

Locally agreed priorities must be kept under constant review. In many localities there are splendid health-education programmes aimed at specific target groups. Because they have proved to be successful, they are maintained and perpetuated, thereby depriving other groups of the possibility of receiving similar attention. Some groups are easily perceived as in need of health education, or in a situation where the provision of such programmes fits comfortably into an existing pattern of activity, such as those attending clubs or schools, those with demonstrable deprivations, those in defined socioeconomic or cultural categories. Other groups in the community may not be so easily defined, or may be considered capable of self-help. This may or may not be realistic, and the priorities of any provision must be reviewed regularly in order to encompass as many groups as possible, and to spread the provision as far as possible. A partnership approach can help to lessen the direct input required of any one professional, and to utilize all inherent skills found within the locality so that health education can be provided on a wide scale, with limited direct commitment from individual professionals but guidance and help as appropriate.

The above aims are very broad and readers will still be in situations where they are directly involved with specific target groups — though it is hoped that it will encourage them to reconsider their approaches within their own practice. Below are a few pointers towards various groups in a variety of settings, and a few related aspects of targeting health education.

Dictionary definitions of 'target' are multiple, the one least evident within service provision is "a sight on a levelling staff". Perhaps it is worth while remembering that the objective of health for all will act as a leveller within society, if it is achieved. When fewer people suffer diseases, discomforts or the results of social or medical deprivation, more people are likely to be well and active. Needs and demands for health education should decrease proportionately, and when the set objective has been reached, health-education efforts will change to provide new information only and to organize maintenance service so that there is no deterioration to "the bad old days". Some planners and practitioners may be concerned that their efficiency and effectiveness may mean that future generations of health educators are no longer needed, and regret this, so unconsciously blocking maximum developments.

Age-related target groups

Different age groups have traditionally received specially structured health-education inputs. It is questionable at which age such input can usefully be started, and even more questionable at which stage the input should become part of professional practice.

Children

Young children are fascinated by their bodies, and this can be channelled towards an awareness of bodily functions and their healthy maintenance. Parents appear the most appropriate people to provide this basic form of health education. Few parents, however, at present have the detailed knowledge to be able to satisfy a child's curiosity. Parents might be encouraged to learn sufficient to teach their children, and go beyond this to consider the health needs of all family members. The information required to help parents is gradually becoming available in book and pamphlet form, but insufficient use appears to be made of already existing teaching media. It is rare that informal groups are guided towards discussion of relevant topics, such as people sitting in dentists, doctors, hospitals or other waiting areas which contain little or uninteresting information. This would provide a captive as well as an interested audience, possibly leading to continuation of learning among those present and moving through a range of health and related matters. It would require that many professionals alter their work styles, using available opportunities rather than planning a set pattern for the day, using flexible hours for work and a different system of accountability to their employers. Working in such a way implies recognition of professionals as independent practitioners, while relying on their professionalism to fulfil their roles and account for their actions.

Parents are often uncertain about details required to satisfy a child's curiosity, and reassurance can provide them with the confidence to increase their own knowledge. Many parents may have received varying information about health matters, from old wives' tales and myths to horror stories and misinterpretation of valid data. They may need to be helped to discern the valid from the erroneous or outdated.

Parents

Therefore, the major target group for any health-education programme which requires observable or measurable outcomes is parents. As parents also form the major group within the adult population, the health-education process can continue as long as it is considered helpful and appropriate. Parents' needs will change as their children grow up. Parents become in-laws and grandparents, are distanced from their children and have to cope with loss and bereavement. Parents' interest is unlikely to be restricted to health matters, and it may be pertinent to draw their attention to relationships between health, environment, housing and employment as well as local, national and international matters. Economic factors will be very much a part of their daily lives. Health education should enable them to relate economic constraints to health, and provide the tools for averting health breakdown through, for example, deficient nutrition. Such education may, of course, alert parents to knowing when danger levels have been reached, and create some militancy, urging improvements which would allow health-related behaviour. No health educator can avoid the danger of creating militancy, as greater awareness of circumstances, improved information and increased knowledge can naturally lead to the desire to alter any part of the circumstances which are not conducive to well-being.

Within any society at present, there are parents who are influenced by a multitude of adverse factors, and who will, therefore, find it difficult to believe that any action of theirs can have an effect on the well-being of themselves or their families. It may be that health educators need to assume a professional advocacy role in such situations, so that the adverse factors can be reduced and, in the long term, overcome. The advocacy role may include accompanying parents to official resource allocators, such as housing officers, ensuring that they are in receipt of appropriate benefits and mobilizing other available helping agencies and resources.

Schoolchildren

Schoolchildren are captive audiences and are the target group for much health-education effort from many professionals and lay educators. It has become an accepted 'truth' that if children and adolescents are taught about health, utilization of health and other services and interpersonal relationships, they, as parents of tomorrow, will be in a position to provide health education to their young children. They will also require less input as adults. This seems very logical, so much so, that it is suspect. There has been health education in many schools for at least a decade, and in some a lot longer, so why are we still apparently at the point where health education originally started? There seem to be a number of reasons. First, and perhaps most important, whereas school is seen by politicians and policy makers as making a major contribution to the formation of a child's character, and it is thought by the same people that the 7 out of 24 hours, 5 days per week, spent in a school building for aproximately 10 years of one's life must be the major educative force, practice and experience show that this is rarely so. Children extract from the curriculum provided for them those aspects they need to pass examinations, or which allow them to be seen to progress without overt trouble, and a few other pieces of information if it is proved to them that they are of use in the short or medium term. They virtually ignore all other parts of any formal curriculum, and will rarely remember anything which does not catch their interest or enthusiasm. The educative forces are, first, the home and therefore parents, second, the neighbourhood and therefore friends and, third, the hidden curriculum of any school and therefore the peer group. Formal health education in schools can only have limited impact. The limitations should provide a challenge to health educators, so that they manipulate teaching–learning situations to present health and related matters as desirable knowledge, and incorporated into life, not just school. The School Health Education Project has sought to allow for this when designing teaching materials, geared for different age groups. These materials and teaching packs are now available to all educational establishments, but their usage remains variable.

Health education in schools goes under many different guises:

preparation for citizenship, civic responsibilities, parentcraft, child development, social sciences, biology and physical education. It can form a small component of the teaching programme, or assume outsize proportions by becoming an examinable entity. It can be studied to GCE level, as CSE, as one subject towards the Duke of Edinburgh Award, as a prenursing course, as part of a first-aid and home-nursing programme and as a special certificated course leading to the award by the National Association of Maternal and Child Welfare. Alternatively it can become a filler of time-tables for those considered unable to benefit from other aspects of school education.

At all examinable levels professional input becomes essential; teachers to fulfil the requirements of the examination syllabus, 'experts' to consider specific aspects contained within the syllabus, and an examiner or assessor who judges how much information has been remembered and assesses the possible value rating of this information. There has, as far as is known, never been any study to see whether knowledge is retained for future use, or whether it is left in limbo until stimulated by need or later professional input. This may mean that those receiving teaching which does not result in an examination are receiving less concentrated input, though their needs may in fact be greater.

Teachers

Teachers in schools and colleges should form an important target group. They are required not only to supply information according to syllabuses and curricula, but to answer questions at any time of the day, about many subjects related to health. Many teachers have not had the opportunity to acquire such knowledge, or the experience of life which would assist them. Their present, substantial needs are likely to increase with the admission of handicapped pupils into ordinary schools. The possibility that they will be required to explain the handicapping condition to other pupils, and that they may have to cope with storage and administration of medicine and drugs, as well as satisfying the differing needs and demands of a greater variety of pupils, creates fear and withdrawal among many. The Education Act 1981 is being implemented, leading to integration of children with special needs into ordinary schools, yet its potential impact has not yet been fully realized by all the professionals involved.

A few teachers have developed expertise in teaching health subjects, but fewer have had opportunity to study health education per se. Since the 1970s there have been changes in teacher training programmes. Many courses offer a health or health-education option. The uptake of this option was small at first, but is increasing. A few fortunate teacher trainees have the opportunity to share learning with trainee health professionals. It is not always clear who teaches the teachers, but health educators could make a greater contribution than at present to this developing field, even though it will ultimately change the nature of professional health-education input in schools.

Health visitors and school nurses, and a few doctors, are active members of some school teams. They should be contributing to the health and education of all schoolchildren and teachers. In many instances they do contribute to a greater or lesser extent to health-education programmes, together with workers from other health or social-work agencies, but it would appear that they have not fully grasped the potential presented to them. All children have health indices—sight, hearing, height, weight and posture—measured by health visitors or nurses at least once during school life. Not all children have received an explanation of what these indices mean, how they relate to their growth and development, whether these indices fall within the range of normality and what each individual can do to improve any index which is below expectation. Where the latter has happened, the response has been very positive, and indications are that learning has been real, and remembered for a long period of time.

It would appear to be part of professional responsibility, in this case the responsibility of health visitors, school nurses and doctors, to use the potential inherent in the situation of developmental assessment and to fulfil their function of promotion of health and health knowledge. These professionals have been equally slow to use health indices and assessment programmes in their contact with parents of schoolchildren. Parents may be invited to attend some sessions, such as medical and nursing check-ups, but rarely is this opportunity used to increase the parents' knowledge of child development and health. Active participation in the child's health assessment should lead to active planning for remedial action, and assist in prevention of deficiencies in siblings or other family members. The incidence of common health hazards in schoolchildren, such as obesity and dental caries, could be reduced dramatically by a more broadly based partnership approach. There is little documented evidence as yet, but some unpublished projects and health records indicate that this is so.

The 1981 Education Act also gives parents the right to receive written information about assessments of a child's special needs, including assessments made by health professionals. It would appear to be the first time that legislation specifies that health education must take place, as the health professional can also be required to explain and elucidate the written information, but it does not yet define the quantity and quality of such effort.

The middle-aged

Middle-life is often forgotten by health educators, perhaps because many professionals are personally caught up in this period. Definitions of middle-age vary, but the accepted definition appears to be between 32 and 65 years of age. Personal preference is for the definition which puts middle-age 10 years away from whatever age one is at present. This age group contains the majority of parents, and most of those in employment, paid or voluntary. Occupational-health services have attempted to make provision, including health education, for many employees. Unfortunately not all employers are able or willing to provide an occupational-health service, and many people spend their working life with minimal contact with health or social services of any sort. Occupational-health nurses have made, and continue to make, a substantial contribution to health education, ranging from prevention of accidents to mental-health education, including among this almost all aspects of physical and emotional well-being. In places where nurses in occupational settings have been able to liaise with health workers in other fields, especially those health workers with a community base, there has been evidence of greater success in promotion and maintenance of health, and achievements in health education. Generic health educators should be aware of the existence and extent of occupational-health services in their locality, and alert possible users to their potential as a resource. The National Health Service, one of the largest employers in the country, has now established the principle that occupational-health services should be available to all its employees, although few appear to utilize the service appropriately as yet, and provision is variable in different parts of the country. Much could be achieved by creating greater awareness of its availability and scope.

In some parts of the country, programmes of preparation for retirement are successfully established. The need for this became evident as many people live longer and some spend as much as 30 or more years retired from paid employment. Many of these people can be enabled to lead active and healthy lives. Present provision is made within health, education, social and voluntary services but is inadequate in most instances. Imaginative approaches to education for retirement may, in future, reduce the need for health and social service care and provision.

The elderly

Elderly people are increasing in numbers in all Western countries, including the United Kingdom. The process of ageing cannot be reversed, but many people could remain well and active, or return to a reasonable range of activities after an episode of ill-health, if they were fully aware how to nurture their health potential. Pensions may appear insufficient to meet all needs, housing may need to be adapted to make it manageable, periodic and practical help may be required, but allowing for all this, elderly people could be taught to maintain their health by more adequate nutrition, by correct use of patent and prescribed medicines, by sufficient and regular exercise and by demonstrating to them that they remain full and useful members of society. Many current health efforts are geared towards alleviating isolation and loneliness among elderly people, and it is often forgotten that elderly people remain individuals and individualists. Some welcome the stimulus of new acquaintances, others prefer the companionship of animals, the majority prefer to exist in the comfort of family, kinship and neighbourhood. Health educators have only begun to make an impact in providing teaching and relevant materials for this group. They have not really begun to educate the general public about the contribution elderly people can make to society, about their needs and how these needs can be met. The challenge is urgent, as all population projections indicate that there will be larger numbers of elderly people and significantly larger numbers of very old people in every community in the future.

Expectant parents

Expectant parents and parentcraft education have been given a high priority by many health educators. Recent reports stress the importance of this group, and there is much pressure, especially political, to increase the effectiveness of prenatal teaching. That there is some value in prenatal teaching and preparation for parenthood cannot be questioned, and it is apparent that this target group would benefit by improved provisions. It does seem questionable, however, to increase provisions for expectant parents at the expense of other groups, without increased resources to achieve broader aims. The barrage of current reports, stressing the needs of expectant parents, and their validity vis-à-vis the needs, expectations and rights of others in the community may require careful scrutiny, and answers may be different in different parts of the country.

Subject-related target groups

In view of the overall objectives for the provision of health education, it may be inappropriate to consider target groups in receipt of subject-based information and knowledge. However, in any community and in most settings, there are likely to be pressures to provide health education which are subject specific. The health educator will have to assess the priority rating of each demand, and provide a service accordingly.

Some demands and perceived needs may arise out of new or unforseen circumstances, and some may arise because new knowledge has become available through research and publication and it appears important to disseminate this information. Other demands may be the result or by-product of other health work, or the consequences of previous inaction or inappropriate actions. The list of subjects is enormous, but a few examples are given below:

1. Unemployment and its effect on health.
2. Preparation for retirement.
3. Use of leisure time.
4. Prevention of coronary heart disease, or the related antismoking, anti-obesity lobby.
5. Prevention of addictions — alcohol, drugs, gambling, etc.
6. Promotion of dental health.
7. Genetic engineering and human life.
8. Health and safety at work.
9. Health hazards in the environment.

Health campaigns

In recent years there have been a number of campaigns, using combinations of health-education inputs, and using the general public or local populations as target groups. It has proved difficult to assess the impact of such wide-spread propaganda, and indications are that there have been very mixed results. The immediate impact has usually been great, and slogans of the campaign have become incorporated into everyday language and usage. There is no evidence to prove that the long- or medium-term impact matches the initial reaction.

The most successful campaign is reported to have been promoting the wearing of seat belts, as part of accident prevention. It used peak-time television as its main medium, with a famous personality giving the message. Audience research found that the campaign had to be repeated at intervals, as within weeks of cessation the number of people wearing seat belts declined again. Each successive phase of the campaign increased the number of people who acquired the habit of wearing belts. Since results were last analysed compulsory seat belt legislation has been introduced, and it will never be clear how much change of behaviour was a voluntary outcome resulting from the campaign, and how much was the avoidance of paying a penalty in law.

The Health Education Council's campaign 'Look After Yourself' appears to have had similar results. Initial impact was great, as indicated by responses to advertisements and requests for brochures and materials. However, it does appear that the impetus has not been maintained at the initial level, and it remains unproven whether there has been any long-term benefit. Proof may, of course, become available in the future.

Antismoking campaigns have been repeatedly launched in recent years, following the 1971 report from the Royal College of Physicians. Initially the number of smokers dropped drastically. There were differences between the groups who responded to the campaign. Doctors by and large supported the official stance and gave up smoking, unconfirmed evidence shows that the impact on nurses was minimal. It would appear from more recent information, though not documented evidence, that smokers are balanced throughout groups in the community, that the number of heavy smokers has been reduced, not through the campaign itself, but through social pressures arising out of the campaign. However, the number of actual smokers appears to be on the increase again, and elements of 'counter-productivity' are becoming evident.

Campaigns as described above are costly, and it could be argued that results do not warrant expenditure. However, if the aim of such campaigns is to increase awareness, rather than change behaviour or alter attitudes, then they may be regarded as both an effective and acceptable expenditure.

Further Reading

Cowley, J (1981) Health Education in Schools, Harper & Row
DES (1977) Health Education in Schools, HMSO
DHSS (1980) Inequalities in Health, Black Report, HMSO
DHSS (1982) The Pattern of Maternity Services, HMSO
Foot, M (1973) Aneurin Bevan, vol. 2, Davis Poynter

Health and Safety Commission (1978) The Way Ahead, Occupational Health Series, HMSO

Health Education Council (1977) Policy Document: The Scientific Basis of Dental Health Education

Mahler, H (1982) The new look in health education, Journal of the Institute of Health Education, 20 (3):5–12

Pugh, G (1980) Preparation for Parenthood, National Children's Bureau

Rathbone, B (1973) Focus on New Mothers, RCN

Royal College of Physicians (1971) Smoking and Health Now, Pitman Medical & Scientific

Thompson, H (1981) Survey into Fathers' Attitudes towards Parentcraft Classes, Johnson & Johnson

CHAPTER 9

HEALTH EDUCATION — THE APEX OF COMMUNICATION

to communicate = to give a share of
= to have something in common with others
= to succeed in conveying one's meaning to others

Chambers Twentieth Century Dictionary (1972)

The art and skill of communicating effectively is to be able to understand meanings, intents and nuances of each other's speech, to enable others to understand the import of one's statements and to do so in a variety of ways and by many different means, supplemented or accompanied by nonverbal means of communication.

Verbal communication, speech, is the acme of communication, as by this means one can not only convey facts and figures but also ideas or ideals and proceed in a constructive, logical manner, individually and in partnership with one or more people. Nonverbal communications can be very varied, and include signs and symbols, body language and, not least of all, grimaces and gestures. Communication technology is developing fast, often with the suspected motive of replacing speech, but also affecting verbal communications by changing language styles and creating slogans which become absorbed into everyday usage.

Letters, communication by correspondence, are being replaced by messages spoken onto tapes or transmitted by telephone. Television speaks to its audience with minimal opportunity of being answered, newspapers present views which may not reflect the whole truth or which try to arouse interest by sensationalism.

During the last decade telephone answering machines have been developed which absolve one from direct communication; business machines, which convey messages across thousands of miles in a few minutes; and computers, which can provide written or pictorial information in seconds. Information technology is moving towards screen-telephones, on which one can see the person to whom one is talking even if they are thousands of miles away, and conferences or meetings can be held via televisions or telephones, installed in private homes and offices. Both the latter ways of communicating may become more economic and comfortable, and therefore productive, than holding meetings in hot stuffy board-rooms. They are already available, but underused. It is wise, therefore, for the health educator to consider all aspects of communication, and to choose those which are most appropriate for the purpose and most readily and economically available. Newer methods can be tried, and may, in time, replace those in current use.

Verbal communication

Verbal messages can pass between higher animals, such as apes and whales, but humans are unique in having developed speech to such an extent that it has become a means in itself. Animals generally use speech to demand something relating to their basic needs, such as food or love, and occasionally to indicate aggression. Humans use speech for the same fundamental needs, but have progressed in its use to express the whole range of emotions, and also to apply a socially acceptable veneer to some of their basic feelings. Human beings have perfected the art of using speech to cover and obscure what they are thinking and feeling, as well as to describe theories, ideas and philosophies. Speech can be used at different levels of sophistication, in a systematic and grammatical way or more haphazardly. Speech exists irrespective of which language is used as the format of expression. Speech can be a cover-up for communication breakdown, in the sense that people may speak at each other without mutual understanding.

Speech or language is a part of normal human development, physical and psychological; the degree to which it is developed will depend on the potential of the person, the environment, stimulation, experience and practice. It can be affected at any time of life by trauma, accident, shock, disease or deliberate design. Medicines, drugs and other chemical substances, as well as constant exposure to excessive noise levels, can have an impact on speech. The noise-level factor does not necessarily relate to 'discos' or other pop sounds, but encompasses industrial environments, for example, airports and factories, and the general level of noise exposure of people living in cities. Particular pitches of sound have more of an impact than others. Hearing may also affect the ability to speak in an acceptable manner; e.g. deaf people may shout, often to the aggravation of those around them.

Speech is fairly well developed by the age of 2½ years, irrespective of which language the child has been exposed to. The range of speech will, of course, depend on the amount of exposure to language at this age. It was thought at one time that the development of speech is dependent upon intelligence, but it now appears that intelligence affects the degree to which speech is used, and the content of any verbal communications. At its normal level, speech allows humans to share their experiences, to demonstrate concern for each other, to make life bearable by exchanging views and news and to create a bond among family members and friends. The bond of speech can be used to generate an in-language shared by a clique, family or group, and so lead to separation of some people from others.

Speech can be used to create images by which people learn. This is the most commonly used method of teaching, and forms the staple of school life. Stories and histories or sagas are structured images which stimulate imagination and encourage thought. Teachers must learn to use speech to maximum effect. Speech can also be formalized, to be repeated in clichés and to form set patterns for the presentation of learned documents, or shaped to make poetry or rhyme. Words within speech act as triggers to memory and thought.

Speech usually identifies a speaker's origins, most districts or regions have special inflections or intonations to vowel sounds. There was a fashion, in the 1950s and 1960s, which suggested that the correct way of speaking English was to speak 'BBC English', a mixture of phraseology and sound produced through the best and worst public schools with a dash of headcold thrown in. The current fashion welcomes regional differences in speech patterns and sounds.

Within speech patterns the use of words is, of course, crucial; most social, work or community groups develop particular patterns which can be used to identify those who belong or who are outside the circle. In this way speech can create barriers, intentionally or unintentionally. This division is often seen to be an identifier of social class, but this is not always the case.

Health educators must learn to use speech in the way most appropriate to achieve their objectives, being aware of the possibilities and dangers, and consciously developing the facility through practice. Conversation is one way of using speech for the benefit of all those participating. It is questionable whether all conversation is effective communication, but it is certainly apparent that conversation, i.e., speech used amongst a group of people who are fairly relaxed and friendly with each other, can lead to messages of interest being passed from one to the other and that it could lead to learning, stimulation and the raising of interest.

Discussion, whichever way the textbooks seek to describe it, appears to be formalized and planned conversation. It should have a similar impact, which can be enhanced by the insertion of information of a definite kind and by introducing new topics at points in the conversational pattern which allow this to be a natural progression. Laughter, or a common cause for amusement, are often spurs to effective discussion. Speech can also be utilized to establish whether the content of the discussion is perceived in the same way by all participants, or whether there is any miscuing.

Speech difficulties, such as stammers, can make the process of communication more difficult. These are not considered here in detail, but in general conversation or discussion such variations and their effect on participants must be accommodated. They can cause disruption or embarrassment, made worse if they are ignored too pointedly or otherwise singled out for attention. It is important not to confuse them with lack of understanding, or allow them to become the butt or centre of attention to the detriment of the matter supposedly under discussion.

Speech can also be used for lecturing, talking at, addressing a large audience or demonstrating degrees of annoyance and dissatisfaction. The content of speech, conversation or discussion may be very substantive and important, though the latter depends on the views of the participants. The sound, tone and pitch of voice may affect communication, as people react to these before they hear or understand the meaning of words. Too loud or too soft, harsh or gentle will all colour the way the content of any verbal message is received. Therefore the way speech is produced is initially as, or more, important than the content. This may change when the participants are familiar with each other, and accept variations as a matter of course.

Speech can, of course, consist of a range of languages, each with their own intonations and relevances. As long as those who wish to communicate use the same language, and are familiar with the meaning of words within that language, the processes of communication remain the same. The greatest problem occurs when people *apparently* speak the same language but where one or other is unaware of differences in meaning. The same problem does not occur when there are obvious language differences, as strategies can be adopted which seek to clarify meaning.

Any health educator in formal contact with individuals or groups must also have self-awareness of repetition of certain words or phrases. It may be the intention to repeat or emphasize some parts of a sentence. On the other hand most people have phases of using a word or phrase repeatedly and monotonously, e.g., 'actually', 'really', 'super', 'to be perfectly frank and honest', etc. Catch phrases can be useful in linking audience and speaker or cause common pleasure and amusement, but they lose value if overused.

Nonverbal communication

Accompanying speech and many other forms of communication are signals, some of which are unconscious, others deliberate. The range of nonverbal communications has only recently been given the attention it deserves, but its impact and pervasiveness should not be underestimated.

Grimaces

Grimaces are innate to human beings, perhaps an inheritance from our supposed ancestors, the apes. Grimaces, prior to or together with speech, can convey a range of feelings and reactions which are usually easily recognizable. Desmond Morris in 'Manwatching' (1977) describes and illustrates grimacing and its meaning together with other forms of nonverbal communications in humans. For the teacher or health worker it is important to be aware of the grimaces he or she may make, and how these can be interpreted by others. If grimaces are seen to contradict what is being said, especially if the grimace and the words originate from the same source, this could lead to dissonance and prove a limiting factor in achieving set goals. However, grimacing can be useful if a message is to be conveyed in a crowded room, when establishing contact with strangers, when words cannot be used at the time a reaction is most appropriate or if the person is too young or otherwise prevented from participating in verbal communications. Grimaces can indicate friendliness, like smiles, disgust or just boredom.

Gestures

Gestures are very much part of communication, some being deliberate, others acquired incidentally; some used intentionally, others as a matter of habit. The child will acquire gestures through parents, siblings and friends as well as perfecting a few of his own, and persons often revert to these familiar forms of expression throughout life. Some gestures reflect nervousness, tension, ease or are particular to specific countries. In this case, care must be taken in interpretation, the same gesture has different meanings in different countries. The various meanings of a handshake are an example, from habit or friendship to sealing a bargain or initiating contest.

The person who wishes to be seen by others as an educator must be aware of his gestures habitually and unconsciously. When one becomes the focus or leader of a group, every movement is observed by someone else, especially when the observed has least time or opportunity to observe the gestures of others. Schoolchildren are well known to mimic any gestures they see, and can mock some. Advantage can be gained if habitual gestures, which one does not wish to alter, are stressed and thereby rendered harmless and acceptable. Gestures are important to emphasize elements of speech, and are often used to elaborate or describe what is being said. This is a very positive aspect of teaching, as visual impact enhances the spoken word and helps retention and memory.

Some gestures do have specific meanings, and do not necessarily accompany speech, such as thumping a table when annoyed, slamming a door, poking one's tongue out or stamping one's foot. They can be extremely effective if used sparingly and in the right situation, but do not usually form part of the health-educator's repertoire.

Body-language and posture

Body-language and posture are both significant nonverbal signals. They indicate mood, feelings and approachability or coolness. A head held erect and a firm step usually indicate confidence, though they can be acquired as part of a protective mechanism; twitching hands or fiddling with objects such as paper or pens indicate stress; downcast eyes or drooping lids signal shyness or distress. Observable changes in posture can provide clues to the person's state of mind and thereby receptivity to information. Constant wriggling in seats by members of an audience usually means boredom or disassociation with what is being said.

Many women, and some men, enhance the effects of body language through hair styles and make-up, and any changes in this can be as significant as language or speech itself. The effectiveness of communication can be greatly enhanced if body language and gestures are used consciously; proximity of chairs and leaning in the direction of the person addressed or the speaker indicate interest or care; eye-to-eye contact shows that one is treating the other person as an equal; nodding or shaking of head are commonly used, shrugs can annoy, and a relaxed posture can help others to relax.

Any or all of these can enhance or mar communication, as nonverbal messages are received parallel to any spoken word, and because their pervasiveness is universal, they can be seen and understood as being fundamentally more important than the intended message of words. Most people react instinctively to nonverbal clues. A smile will normally draw a smile in return or at least make verbal approaches possible, and professional distancing can be avoided.

Social skills training

During teacher training in the United Kingdom, and some other forms of professional training, social skills form part of the curriculum. In health-visitor or nurse education courses this may appear in the guise of interview techniques, in management courses this may be part of personnel functions. In many institutions of further and higher education methods of teaching and learning are used which demonstrate the use persons can make of themselves as a communication tool. Video-tapes and other visual aids have made this possible.

In the postregistration School of Nursing in one part of France, classrooms have been fitted with mirrors on the two longest walls so that students can constantly observe their gestures, grimaces and other nonverbal behaviour. Occasionally this is used for formalized social skills training, but mostly it is used to create awareness and allow modification of behaviour to take place voluntarily. Student groups who use these classrooms consist mostly of clinical teachers/ward sisters and public-health nurses.

Dress and costume

Dress and costume are also nonverbal means of communication. Costume can signify the country of origin, such as Welsh hats, or kilts from any of the gaelic regions, the pattern of the tartan having most significance and indicating country as well as clan. Most commonly used in this way are uniforms, which identify the functions and status of the wearers and signal to others the respective roles, such as saluting, attitudes of superiority or subservience, possible quality and quantity of interactions. Uniforms may provide protection and give confidence to both wearer and those who identify role and status; they often limit the range of expectations and initiatives because they delineate the parameters of action. Suits worn at formal interviews form another traditional category of dress, turbans or saris openly declare membership of a religious group or ethnic category.

Teenagers are proud of their 'pop' gear, which declares them to consider themselves members of a particular section of their environment. School uniforms are a separate case though they lead to easy identification of the wearer.

Sudden changes in dress style may be significant in openly declaring the personal development of an individual towards a particular goal, or they may reflect the mood of the present, a need to provide some cheer and uplift through physical changes. At one time the colour of clothes was significant, but this is no longer any sort of accurate guide; any colour or mixture of colours have become acceptable. There are more and varied materials available, their range and nature have helped to break down inhibitions and traditions, and their relative cheapness no longer requires the majority to select long-lasting and hard-wearing fabrics. Colours can, however, occasionally provide nonverbal signals in identifying members of some groups, but even within those groups there is not always strict adherence to the significant colour, e.g., black, dark grey or mauve worn by clergy, yellow worn by members of an Eastern religious sect, black for mourning or widowhood, and white for virginity — especially at weddings. Blue has always indicated a depressive mood, and it has also signified the wearer to be a member of the Navy, police force or nursing!

The significance of clothing and costume as a means of nonverbal communication is real, but is not totally reliable or applicable in all situations. Some people would dress very differently if they had access to a range of clothes, others cannot afford to change or be fashionable because of economic constraints.

Signs, signals and symbols

Signs, signals and symbols are yet other aspects of nonverbal communication. Everyone is familiar with signs made by gesturing; some groups have agreed signs and signals to obviate or lessen the need for verbal or written messages. Signs and signals can be a very effective means of communication, but only if the partners to the process agree to the meaning of each signal, and if they are always used in the same way. Deaf people can communicate almost entirely by sign language, but there are at least four formal sign languages which are taught at different centres for the deaf, and deaf people may face the problem of having difficulties in communicating with each other as well as with those who would normally use hearing as a part of communication. Symbols can become signs and signals, but they constitute a part of a formal network of communication. The Department of the Environment commissioned several studies on the use of symbols, and has used some of the results in the commonly seen signs in shops, offices, packaging of goods, and in parks, on roads and wherever people, who may or may not speak the same language, congregate. The symbols representing footpaths, toilets and other amenities are the most commonly found examples. The sign for a handicapped person, or access for wheelchairs, has almost become universal. Health education in general appears to have shied away from symbolism, and perhaps this is an area worthy of development. It could be specially useful when teaching children, who not only find it easy to understand symbols, but who thoroughly enjoy them. Medicine uses many symbols, most of which are little understood by outsiders. A very common symbol, used by many professionals is the ♀ for males and ♂ for females — or is it the other way about? Most people know the signs, but not which is which.

Listening

Listening is a vital component of effective communication. It is a skill and an art. The skill of listening has to be learned in the same way as all other skills, and the art has to be perfected through conscious effort and practice. Listening is not only hearing words actually used, but also understanding their overt and hidden meanings; of giving total attention, however fleeting, to the speaker; of showing interest and respect for others' views and opinions. Respect creates an enabling climate, and could make the speaker more receptive when next addressed. Respect also creates self-confidence and provides reassurance of personal worth, both implicit aims of health education. Listening as an art form enables the creation and effective use of personal space, a space which many people lack; it allows the speaker facility to verbalize thoughts, and clarify varying strands of information. A part of the art is to utilize pauses, not by filling them with words, but by allowing them to be generators of fellow-feeling and peace or appreciation. Creative silence can be supportive as well as therapeutic or healing.

Most professionals consider themselves 'good listeners', but few have perfected the art. It is extremely difficult to use effectively, because silence can be felt as a threat to authority and there is often the urge to fill the gap. There is an element of fear on the part of professionals, a residual feeling of impotence. Professionals, especially nurses, have been trained to be 'up and doing', and there may even remain a suspicion that listening is a waste of time professionally. Professionals rated most highly by their clients are those who listen attentively, allow pauses and silences, make friendly gestures at the right moment and speak relatively little, but in a way most acceptable to the hearer. Responses made taking into account what they have heard, as well as what they have observed and divined whilst listening, are most favourably received, and are more likely to lead to subsequent action.

Written communication

More people receive their health education through written than spoken words. Apart from health education in the mass media, which is discussed in Chapter 10, there is a plethora of written material purporting to provide health information, including pamphlets, booklets, comic strips and books. The difficulty is that reader and writer often interpret and understand the words and sentences very differently. There is no opportunity for dialogue, for questions and answers, for elaboration or for making written material relevant and suitable for each individual consumer. Once written, and even more so once printed, written communications cannot be amended or enhanced. Every document has a limited life, it gets out of date, is superceded, or no longer relevant. This is the built-in frustration of this form of communication. It may be complete and valid at the time of production, but requires attention when it may not be possible to give it the thoughts it deserves, or when the writer has moved on from the original information, either physically or mentally. Some aspects of relevance to health education practice are mentioned below, though these are by no means exclusive.

Letters

Personal letters are difficult to write, and communicating with a varied clientele by this means can be hazardous. Too much formality creates antipathy, too much informality can create suspicion. Letters must state their purpose, but also contain details of importance to the recipient; for example, when someone is invited to participate in a health-education programme they may require to know date, time and place of meetings, the length of any proposed session — this is vital in the case of parents who have to collect children from school, or for people who have to provide a service or run a business — the number of planned sessions, i.e., the length of possible commitment, and who, apart from themselves, has received a similar invitation. The latter is easily overlooked; for example, Elizabeth Perkins (1975) found in her studies of parentcraft teaching that fathers would have liked to attend, but often did not do so because they assumed that they might be the only male present.

Publicized programmes should be clear and precise and every effort should be made to meet the expectations created. Most people wish to be aware of the nature of the contact they are likely to have, whether they are coming for a 'chat', to be talked at, to see a film or to listen to an eminent guest.

Reports

Reports of activities may be required for many purposes, such as management audit, evaluation or, most importantly, sharing the experience with those unable to attend. Formal reports usually follow a set pattern: there is need to be precise, concise, separate data from professional opinion and judgement, and make valid points strongly and lucidly, in a way most acceptable to the recipient. Managers and treasurers usually require any report to be based on figures, whereas professionals may consider that numbers do not reflect the nature or essence of their activities. This should be made clear, and the relevant information provided additionally to any necessary statistics. Reports need not be a response to requests, but can be the catalyst for future actions.

Reports or statements sent to the press and other forms of mass media are often subject to alteration before being placed before the public. They, therefore, require special clarity and often the sort of brevity which would make it impossible for an editor to alter the meaning. Too few reports of successful professional activities receive general publication, except for articles in professional journals. Most of those for general consumption describe problems and difficulties or gaps in meeting public demands. Health-education activities may receive more recognition if practitioners published their successful outcomes — blowing one's own trumpet is not always detrimental.

Record keeping

Record keeping is the bane of most professionals' lives. It is, however, an important facet of professional responsibility, and has to be accepted as the more tedious part of the task. Records are important as they are used for resource allocation, decisions about staffing levels and forward planning. Records may be useful for assessing the range of activities which are necessary at individual and community levels, for determining needs, and for noting changes which may affect the practice or alter the composition of the clientele, e.g., a significant rise in any age group within the population, repeated demands for a particular facility or lack of use of another. Where and if forms provided for the majority of essential records do not meet the criteria seen as appropriate by practitioners, they can affect change by making written suggestions for alteration and amendment.

Most professionals are also employees and, therefore, they must be accountable. A summary of their actions, activities and judgements is contained in records and reports. Those who are not in paid employment are still accountable to their clientele and to the profession to which they belong, in that they should document their range of practice, their objectives and how, when and whether these have been achieved. There are legal aspects to record keeping and report writing which have been most clearly demonstrated in the field of nonaccidental injury. The Health Visitors Association published a book which, whilst the title is specific — 'The Law and Health Visitors' — could provide useful pointers to anyone working in the health and social services field (Burr, 1982).

Other factors

Communication processes do not begin and end with the points made above. A number of other factors need to be taken into account:

Memory. Few people can remember all that they have been taught or have learned, most will attempt to memorize those pieces of information which are of special interest to them, irrespective of their relevance, or those bits which appeal to them and which they consider important. Informal methods of teaching and learning appear to stimulate memory to a greater extent than formal lectures or set pieces. Any form of participation increases the ratio of remembering to forgetting. Educational theory suggests that approximately 50% of all that is learned is stored in memory, though it may be as low as 33% initially, the latter figure being enhanced by effort, reinforcement and relevance or need. It has also been shown that there can be blocks to memory, for example, expectant parents cannot remember much of any prenatal teaching relating to the period following the arrival of the new infant (Clulow, 1982).

Memory can be encouraged by *reinforcement*. This may be another word for repetition, but could mean presenting the same message in different formats and by different methods, and by creating facility and opportunity for recall to take place. Occasionally it may be appropriate to reinforce messages by means of a reward system, such as stars given to pupils, but this has to be limited if the essence of health education is considered.

Memory and reinforcement are aided if any message has more than one format. Spoken and written words can be enhanced by visual materials, posters, pictures, films, slides and demonstrations. A range of materials is available. The size of the Health Education Index (1982), when compared with previously published indexes, shows this clearly. There should be little need for the health educator to prepare materials, unless that is part of their particular function, but there may be every need for the generally available materials to be adapted for local or particular use. Visual impact is enhanced if the imagery is clear, colourful and shows situations which are familiar or attractive to the viewer. Cartoons are an excellent medium, but they should be simple and gentle, rather than rollickingly funny — not everyone's sense of humour is the same. It is helpful if visual aids can be used for repetition or revision, many films have a deeper impact when seen the second time, but there is a time when repetition becomes counterproductive.

Planning for health education should include consideration of the expectations of the recipient, his previous experience and possible exposure to health education, the strengths and limitations of the facilities which are operative, including the experience and expertise of the provider, expectations of outsiders and colleagues and the influence and effect the presence of an observer may have, if not everyone present is an active participant. That the size and nature of the group is taken into consideration is taken for granted.

Most forms of communication have been tried by health educators, there is little evidence to prove which have been most effective and why. The most important suggestions for success to emerge from the scanty evidence are:

1. Any method is worth trying, and often worth repeating with adaptations.

2. A nonpressurizing and nonprescriptive approach has the most observable long-term results.

3. Participation in planning, provision and evaluation by educator and educated lead to continuance of interest and in turn create further, but realistic, demands.

To date not many of the newer forms of resources and technological equipment are readily available to health educators in the United Kingdom, but they should be incorporated as soon as possible. Apart from a computer doing the planning and evaluation, it would be a pleasure to hear a hit record made by a group of health educators extolling the value and virtue of health or to see video games which award points to the most knowledgeable about health matters and services. Cartoons are used widely overseas.

Enthusiasm and perseverance are the essential qualities for health education practitioners. Achievement of objectives and other observable results should lead to the maintenance of enthusiasm, and serve as the most valid encouragement to continue.

There is a distinct need for health educators to publish their successes and less successful attempts, to communicate them to colleagues and others who are interested or involved. More public description of various practices and the rationale for them, as well as the results achieved, could avoid wasting resources and manpower on futile endeavours and lead to recognition and establishment of good and reputable practices.

Further reading

Bligh, D (1971, 1972) What's the Use of Lectures? Direct Design Products, Bournemouth

Burr, M (1982) The Law and Health Visitors, Edsall, for the Health Visitors Association

Clulow, C (1982) To Have and to Hold, Aberdeen University Press

Morris, D (1977) Manwatching — A Field Guide to Human Behaviour, Triad Panther

Perkins, E (1975–1980) Ante-natal Education and Preparation for Parenthood, series of 5, Nuffield Health Education Project, University of Nottingham

Wise, A (1965) Communication in Speech, Education Today Series, Longmans

Young, A (1983) Legal Problems in Nursing Practice, Harper & Row

CHAPTER 10

HEALTH EDUCATION AND THE MASS MEDIA

"Be realistic, ask for the impossible"

Graffiti

Mass media are pervasive forces within today's society. Everybody has access and some exposure to one or other element of the media. Many people believe implicitly that what is printed must be true, or that current affairs programmes, news broadcasts and documentaries present up-to-date information and knowledge sufficient to satisfy all needs. Other people claim that they remain totally unaffected by media influences. Both these are extremes of view. Not all that is printed can be truth as seen from different points of view; few people can remain unaffected by media influences, as they most probably receive media-generated information through other people. Much of the effect of media coverage is subtle.

It must be stressed that there are many responsible journalists and broadcasters whose intent is to use the medium honestly and to beneficial effect, who would like it to be a source of education in the broadest sense and who report on health matters because they feel that this can make a useful contribution to the health of the nation or to alleviating shortfalls. People within the media are very aware of possible hazards and misunderstandings, and attempt to overcome these. They have also been the supporters and initiators of audience research, which should provide useful tools for better communications, and whose findings could help all those who have to communicate as part of their professional tasks. Unfortunately the good influences are not always apparent, or are missed by the casual reader, listener or watcher. Decisionmaking teams with responsibility for distribution and circulation or programme planning do not always include a spectrum of expertise and interests.

Mass media suffer similar constraints as other spheres of activity such as

115

shortages of manpower and resources and a few specific ones, such as shortage of time to produce the best articles or films, technical hitches in printing and production, or lack of suitable specialist guidance. Additionally they hold a brief to be immediate in impact, and can be overtaken by the urgency of news or events. They also face the difficulty of being acceptable to a very wide audience with no facility to respond.

The introductory quote to this chapter indicates, however, that programme planners, and editors, are receptive to ideas and opinions, and will usually endeavour to meet proven needs. The biggest challenge for health educators who wish to use mass media is the cost factor. The demand and competition for the best spaces and the written or spoken words as produced by professional health workers are usually interpreted and altered for general consumption, or even curtailed to fit the pattern of a page. This may change intended meanings and cause some concern to practitioners.

Newspapers

Newspapers reach almost every member of the population in the United Kingdom. One paper may be used by a number of readers, and a range of newspapers are available in public libraries. The level of journalism within any given paper, or the views expressed, may be biased towards particular economic or political goals, and items presented are likely to reflect the underlying philosophy of the editorial board. Because papers are produced daily or weekly, they have to concentrate on happenings within society during that period in time, and those events which are dramatic. They therefore have limited facility for long-term projects. Most papers do have sections which deal with health and social aspects of daily living, and many have editors and journalists with special responsibility to write on health subjects. With some notable exceptions, they concentrate on health matters discussed in Parliament or reported as 'dangerous' by special interest groups or environmentalists. One reason why journalists do not cover health education more regularly is that they have no access to information which would make this possible. Health educators should acquire the function of providing up-to-date and relevant information to reporters. Many papers do have a columnist who will write appropriate articles from time to time, but only if he or she has easy access to relevant information, which is geared towards the interests of the readership and can be made to sound stimulating.

Many papers have a letter page. It is noticeable that a large number of letters seek information about health matters or resources, and this could demonstrate a need for more specific health education. The respondent to letters received by a paper acts as a generalist health educator, and may find it helpful to have access to accurate and professional advice, and someone who would help in extracting those letters which indicate need for follow-up actions. There are some people who use letter pages to get a 'second opinion', i.e., to see whether public advice matches the information already received.

Local newspapers have different pressures to national ones, and many reflect health needs and demands of their readership. In recent years many local papers have made a substantial contribution to the spread of information, notifying their readers about local facilities and describing professional roles and spheres of activity. They are rarely in a position where they can commission this material, but will give any material sent to them due consideration. How many health educators, and how many nurses and health visitors, use this vehicle through being regular contributors to their local paper, and by submitting articles or letters for publication? How many know their local reporter and talk to him or her when they wish to disseminate information on a wide basis? Such contacts could prove worth while and lead to a speedier and more successful achievement of health-education goals.

There are a few papers and journalists who disparage health education, mainly because it is seen as infringing personal freedoms and liberties, or because its importance is not appreciated. Health educators often complain among themselves about this; how many have tried to contact the persons concerned and explain what their objective is and the reasons behind the objective, stressing the goal of increasing personal freedom and choice, as well as personal health status, by enabling informed decisionmaking? It is more than likely that co-operation would be enhanced by such contacts.

Magazines and journals

Magazines and journals are also widely read. The difference between them is not distinct, but usually magazines could be considered to be of general interest and appeal, while journals are subject- or leisure-interest specific. The range of both is enormous. In general, magazines are prepared to publish articles the editorial board considers of interest or value to their readership. Any submitted article is likely to await its turn before being printed, as content planning is usually some weeks or months ahead of production date. The aim, therefore, has to be at medium- or long-term impact, as compared with materials provided for newspapers. Women's magazines publish many health-related subjects, e.g., slimming diets, household management and personal care. Most editors of women's magazines are interested in receiving appropriate material. Some magazines may pay for contributions published.

Every magazine of this kind has a letters page which could be used by health educators. Most women's and teenage magazines also have 'agony' columns, dealing specifically with personal and health problems and questions. These columns have the widest readership of any part of the magazine. The volume of correspondence received by most magazines is reported to be vast, and health-related questions and difficulties have not altered significantly through recent years, except for freer expression and changing climates of opinion and fashions.

The content of these requests and pleas for help indicates that many people have not received adequate health information, or are unaware of local resources and services. The respondents fulfil an educative function. Some, like Claire Rayner of women's magazines and TV fame, are nurses, others are writers who may have an interest in people or who may have been designated to the job. The latter require knowledge and information, or access to each, before they can adequately fulfil their brief. Many more health educators should be advisors to editorial boards of such magazines.

Special interest journals

Special interest, including leisure interests, journals are unlikely to carry health information, unless the subject matter is health related. There may, however, be an opportunity for professional input as many deal with topics which should have a safety angle. Editors are unlikely to request information which is not subject-specific, so the onus is on the health educator to make the first approach and some positive suggestions.

Professional journals form a small proportion of the total available. Some editors of such journals do not receive sufficient material of the right nature and calibre. This used to be true of nursing journals, though there has been a significant change during the past decade. Most professional journals provide the prospective writer with information on how to produce their scripts in the specific style and format of the journal.

Commercial firms, such as companies selling products for babies, publish news-sheets. Professional contribution to such news-sheets is usually requested, and should be given, even if the professional's recommendation of the firm's products proves to be contrary to commercial interests. Objective assessment of products in such cases may help consumers, other professionals and the company who may seek to make their product more acceptable. Most health authorities have now established ethics committees who can advise on the hazards and desirability of involvement with any commercial concern.

The number of magazines depicting violence, horror or pornography is reported to be increasing, causing serious concern to many professionals as well as the general public. Health educators have to decide whether it is part of their professional responsibility to make representation against certain publications or against availability and access to them. They may be unable to make the decision until there is valid evidence that these publications are harmful.

Radio

Radio has been with us a long time, and its use and influence has changed substantially through the years. At one time people listened to a limited number of stations, but there is now a much wider choice, and there is active competition with television, video recordings, music-centres and other home entertainments. Most major radio stations have always included incidental health education; a big increase in immunization take-up occurred when characters in a popular radio serial decided it was a good thing. 'Mrs Dale's Diary', 'Waggoners Walk' and similar series were as or more influential than, for example, the Radio Doctor. Each new series acquires a large and devoted following. Programme planners often seek professional advice on health-related content, but have difficulty in identifying the most appropriate expertise available to them. Suggestions for the inclusion of topical health issues are usually welcome, especially if they are backed by names of possible participants. Broadcasters prefer to be alerted to inaccuracies prior to going on the air, but also welcome subsequent comments.

Panels of experts are often invited to answer questions in phone-in programmes and to discuss topical issues. Some health workers have participated in these programmes and shown that they are more than capable of making a valuable contribution. Many more should in future be ready to take part.

Local radio stations often give air-time to health-related issues, and have given health workers the opportunity to be interviewed. They have done much to increase awareness of professional roles and functions within the community. To be interviewed on radio can be nerve-racking, but interesting, and the impact could be very far-reaching. Most local radio stations do not have the time or staff to seek out health professionals, but are glad to be informed of events in their locality, or of people willing to join in appropriate programmes.

Recently special interest stations have developed, health educators should be ready to utilize this new opportunity, especially as it is likely to reach those groups who do not attend clinics or any other official venue for health or education. It is probable that some stations will be broadcasting in a limited area, similar to a health visitor's 'patch', but others will range more widely.

Whilst, in general, fewer people listen to a smaller selection of programmes, much information is passed from listener to family, friends and neighbours, and can stimulate interest and attendance at more formal sessions. The past had its Radio Doctor, the 1980s and 1990s could have its Radio Nurse, Radio Health Visitor and Radio Health Educator. Some nurses have joined radio panels, and have proved themselves very able and acceptable to the public. Their contribution has also compared favourably with that of medical colleagues, who are more experienced in public relations work.

1983 saw the first series of programmes on radio and television entitled 'Well-woman', specifically designed to inform and improve the health status of women.

There are a number of medical programmes on radio and television which range beyond treatment and cure. They often describe developments in medicine, and occasionally stray into the area of health education. The effectiveness of the latter could be enhanced by active involvement of practising health educators. It is sometimes difficult for the ordinary professional to be accepted, especially by planning teams. The level of contribution of experts is often overestimated. Practitioners of health education have to become more positive in their approaches, and not wait to be asked for their services, but offer them unsolicited, either as programme advisers or as participants.

Citizen-band radio is now commonplace and legal. It is used by people who wish to strike up friendships, who may be lonely, who are travelling or who are at home, but who may be unaware that they may have health needs. The maintenance of their health and happiness should be a challenge to health educators, and a health input could be made with minimum effort and the opportunity utilized with maximum effect.

Television

Television is often much maligned as the interrupter of family life, the destroyer of conversation, the creator of violent reactions as well as a time waster. Generally programme planners attempt to present a mixture of entertainment, education, information and topical or sports programmes. One part of the 1979 conference held by the National Association for Maternal and Child Welfare concentrated on television, and it became evident that contributors were convinced of its educational value, but also aware that full potential has not yet been reached. It was urged that individuals should be censors of what they wished to receive on their screens. The channel selection button's use is reflected in viewing statistics, and if the *off* knob is used too frequently, speedy amendments occur to attract more viewers.

Television programmes can be a substantive educative force. Many medical and health-orientated programmes are superbly produced, and are available for hire. Many programmes discuss health-related issues, rather than specific topics. There are constraints which require decisions on how much of a subject to include, e.g., viewing time, competition for peak hours showing, length of available schedule and presentation. The best designed and photographed programme can fail to achieve its objective if the presenter is unacceptable to the audience or acts as an irritant. Watching television can be a solitary pastime, stifling conversation and become all absorbing; it can also be turned into a stimulant for conversation and family activity. Selectivity and moderation appear to be the best guides to successful watching.

Programme planners ask whether the impact of their presentations is long term or transient. It would appear that impact is likely to be transient unless reinforced by repetition with suitable spacing, subsequent discussion and the additional input of professionals at field level. There also appears to be a lack of dissemination of information of programme content. Both BBC and IBA publish a year's programme, listing educational and health-educational schedules, many months ahead of transmission. These booklets do not have as wide a currency as they deserve, and they could usefully form a resource for health educators.

Health education on television is usually considered in the context of 'serious' or specially designed programmes. This is just one possibility. Entertainment could well be used to transmit health information. After all, to be healthy should be fun. Why not have fun in acquiring and maintaining health? 'The Angels', based in a hospital, is a very popular series at peak viewing times, but many opportunities for incidental health education have been missed. Such input would not interfere with the nature of the series, or the stories running through it. Other long-running series could be equally useful vehicles for health information. Incidental learning is often more effective and better retained than specially designed and directed input.

So far health professionals have participated in a limited way only in planning, direction and transmission of relevant programmes. Opportunity to be more actively involved could be created, and should be grasped. One dilemma with health and other messages sent via any of the mass media is that they reach interested persons second or third hand and get distorted in the process. Mr A reads an article or watches a programme, he relates his experience to a friend, who tells a neighbour who tells a friend and so on until the message is totally unrecognizable. Health educators often have to break into this cycle and disentangle the resulting confusion, being alerted through members of their client groups that received information has been misinterpreted. This can be difficult if the professional has not seen or heard the original programme. It may be impossible for professional practitioners to listen or see the majority of relevant programmes, but a colleague group could arrange for coverage amongst its members.

Another dilemma is that none of these media can elicit an immediate response, despite efforts at audience participation, and, therefore, there is little provision for resolving any misunderstandings. Many people watch television as a matter of habit, rather than choice or planning, and may catch a part of a programme only. They, therefore, receive only a small part of the total message, and may misinterpret it through lack of detail. Health educators have to be aware of this dilemma and be prepared to overcome any misunderstanding. Broadcasts by the Open University are a good illustration. Many OU courses concern themselves with health-related subjects, but the radio and television components are closely linked to the written text. Some programmes are self-sufficient and self-explanatory, but others can easily be misunderstood, or misapplied, if not seen as part of the total course and supplemented by detailed information and discussion.

Advertising

Advertising is another pervasive medium. Most mass media contain some form of advertising material. Papers and magazines rely on advertising revenue for their existence; the IBA gets a high proportion of its revenue from advertising; the BBC does not accept advertising, but there is often incidental advertising contained in sets and props. Advertising has a specific aim, i.e., to interest people in a particular product or brand and to stimulate them to buy it. There are voluntary codes of practice for advertisers, but many do run contrary to the aim of health education.

Some people consider that advertising can have undesirable consequences. Certainly most advertisements are pleasant to look at, colourful and attractive; if seen often enough, they will be absorbed unconsciously leading to product recognition. The majority of people regard advertisements, especially those on television, as one form of entertainment. However, there are people who can be tempted beyond their means to try any new product or bargain offer, and may suffer as a result. There are also people who see advertisements as presenting the material goods they are unable to obtain, and it could lead to greater discontent, unhappiness and jealousy.

Advertisements are likely to get more subtle and attractive in future. Health education may need to acquire the additional function and skill of applying realism to the dream world represented by advertisers. Health educators also have a duty to ensure that advertisements do not display obviously harmful substances, and may need to apply pressure to halt such displays and to correct any misinformation given to the public.

The cost of advertising is high and, therefore, out of the reach of most health educators, with the exception of those participating in national or local campaigns. Ideally health education should be able to advertise itself in a similar way to commercial products. Advertisers can teach health educators the best way to reach a large number of people, and the methods used could be applied to the promotion of health.

Telephones

Telephones have been with us for so long that they are regarded as a utility, and their potential for use in health education is often forgotten. The telephone is a communication tool to provide links between two speakers. In reality, it can be used to reach a substantial number of people at one time. Commercial concerns use this potential to sell products, and their agents use the telephone directory to contact customers and increase sales.

Telephone conferences and teaching/learning sessions are now possible. Up to 20 people can be linked by telephone. This is a comfortable means of listening and talking, and does not lead to stresses of travelling or leaving home and children unattended. It also limits time involved. There is a cost factor which may mitigate against use for teaching purposes, but it is one medium which could be utilized in selected situations.

Telephones have been used successfully to provide emergency and advisory services, such as Samaritans and Family Network. They can be a medium for health education, although their full potential has so far largely been ignored by professionals.

Professional health-education contribution to mass media has to date been on individual basis, using one expertise at a time. The possibility of co-operative effort, by producing, perhaps, whole programmes or writing articles together, has only been rarely used. By co-operation and concerted effort the influence on media output could become very substantial, and would cover a broader perspective than any one person could provide. It would also enhance the totality of efforts.

With the advent of Teletext, Oracle, and other uses of the microchip, possibilities for using mass media for health education become limitless.

Further reading

Bloomfield, R and Follis, P (1974) The Health Team in Action, BBC Publications

Jones, C (1979) Parents, children and programmes. In Does Provision Meet the Need?, Report of Conference held by The National Association of Maternal and Child Welfare, 1979, NAMCW, 1 Audley Street, London W1.

CHAPTER 11

RESOURCES FOR HEALTH EDUCATION

It is important to watch that more efficiency does not result in less effectiveness in a wider sense, not only in hospitals, where the main casualties of streamlining may be humanity and convenience, but also in general practice and community care.

R. G. S. Brown, (1973) the Changing National Health Service,
Routledge & Kegan Paul

Resource allocation has many facets and contexts — political, manpower, methods and scope. This chapter is concerned with the physical resources available to health educators, and the contributory mental resources needed to utilize, organize and extend them. As with any other aspect of health education the discussion cannot be exhaustive. Hopefully new resources will be discovered at many levels and their use and value communicated to colleagues and other interested people. Some resources will continue to be the backbone of health teaching, and change will depend on attitudes among resource allocators and managers and pressure, proof and argument from those requiring improved resources. Resources do appear to be subject to Parkinson's law; there are never enough; where they are reasonable in quantity they may lack quality; and as soon as a level of adequacy has been achieved, there are new developments which require additional materials and support services. One general problem with physical resources is that obsolescence means loss in value, and it is often impossible to regain anything from the initial expenditure or to exchange old material for new. It is also a sad fact that in some instances there are ample resources available for use, but no or little use is actually made of them. This has acted as a deterrent to resource allocation, and should be carefully considered before making official requests.

The health educator as a resource

The greatest and most plentiful resource available to the general public and service management alike is the individual. Each professional or volunteer has strengths and expertise to bring to the tasks. Each also has special interests which may contribute to the total. Many people also have special skills which do not obviously relate to the task in hand, but which can contribute towards achieving objectives for teaching.

Self-confidence is the boon and the bane of health-education practice. The boon, because it is the resource which acts as the trigger for action, the means of putting plans into operation, and the impetus to move forward with or irrespective of prevailing conditions. The development and maintenance of confidence is the motive power which can make health education a continuous process, and lead to ever greater achievements. Self-confidence should be based on self-knowledge, and be developed proportionately to the development of knowledge and skills. There are those who believe that humility is the greatest asset; self-confidence does not exclude other qualities, including humility if that is appropriate, but is based on a realistic assessment of capabilities, and a periodic reappraisal of all the qualities and skills possessed. Self-confidence does not equate with pride, though it may lead to pride in achievements. Self-confidence is also a bane, because many practitioners have been socialized into presenting themselves as being very confident. This applies especially to professionals with a nursing background. They have acquired a veneer of confidence, which has led to a belief in their own prowess not based on the assessment and reappraisal previously mentioned. It can, therefore, be a dangerous surface quality, which could lead to disillusion and trauma.

The individual can be a resource in many different ways, by carrying out each task well and using initiative in extending the parameters of any role when necessary;. by being in possession of specialist expertise and knowledge; by assisting those not in possession of the same degree of expertise; and sometimes just by being there. In the same way as there are a variety of resources, a person can be used in a variety of ways.

Professional expertise as a resource

Inherent in being a professional practitioner, whether nurse, social worker, environmental health officer or doctor, is that one has a reservoir of knowledge, skills and experience acquired through education, training and practice within one's profession. Added to this should be the life-skills and social skills perfected over a period of time. Together these make a resource pool, which can legitimately be tapped by employers and public, and which is used during one's professional life. Even those who are sceptical about professionals as a group, or resent the fact that some people have been able to amass specialist knowledge and skills, admit that the strengths contained within this pool are tremendous. One resulting responsibility is to share some of the content, and the critics' real criticism is that not sufficient sharing is taking place, keeping professional expertise intact and remote from general access. Each profession makes a unique contribution to the total, all caring professions will have to move closer to sharing a common core of knowledge and resources for health education.

The concept of teamwork arises out of the recognition that a sharing of professional resources could lead to concerted attack on some of the causes of ill-health, and could change the nature of caring tasks and demands which, in turn, would change many aspects of professional practice. Teamwork is an ideal concept, which is achievable with effort and continuous development. In those places where it is less successful, it may be due to a guarding of professional privileges, a fear that roles may be eroded, unrealistic concerns about confidentiality and suspicion of others' roles and contributions.

Confidentiality is an overrated issue of many dimensions. No professional would breach personal confidences without permission of the individual or group concerned, but all caring professionals can share their approach to problem-solving and the principles which govern their work. The aims are usually similar, though the roads to achievement may vary. Additionally confidentiality is often given disproportionate status in the context of professional work, few records are inaccessible, few sites for health care are private and few items of information are of such a nature that they cannot be shared, especially if they are depersonalized.

The pool of professional expertise is, therefore, the greatest resource available within the community, and should be used with increasing effect and concerted teamwork towards the common goal of health education.

The client or lay helper as a resource

Many people see health education as a professional task. It can be argued that health education is a task inherent in the work of every caring professional, but that they cannot achieve any permanent results if they function in isolation. Achievements will also be minimized if professionals

,o not work in partnership with the recipients of health-education messages. Clients, like professionals, bring to health education a range of expertise, knowledge, skills and experience. They bring sets of attitudes which may make them receptive to health teaching, and they may also bring information which could assist in the education of other members of their group and the professionals. Education is a continuous process, not the learning or teaching which occurs at one session or interview, and a partnership approach can ensure that all participants can benefit. The resources within clients can be used to extend practice, by acknowledging and incorporating them in all phases of the health-education process (Figure 5). They can also be used actively, in the priority ratings within any given set of sessions, and giving clients' expertise full recognition by full and active participation. This encourages personal development of clients, and in the long term leads to less direct professional involvement. The resources within client groups have not yet been fully tapped, and it may be of value to health educators to give further consideration on how to utilize the potential of their groups, how to gain from the expertise inherent in the groups and the ultimate relief from work pressures this could entail.

Resources within the National Health Service

Most resource personnel, apart from clients, are Health Service personnel: nurses, midwives, health visitors, doctors and others, and their numbers are increasing. Each person may actually spend less time in patient or client contact as a result of extending roles and reduction in working hours, but each professional within this number should also be able to channel individual resources into achieving maximum results with minimum effort. The pool of professional and lay resources which is available for health education is contained within, or aligned to, the National Health Service.

The National Health Service was created to provide equal opportunity for everybody in the United Kingdom to reach optimum health, whether this high point is in "... the physical, mental and social well-being, not merely the absence of disease ...", or whether it is at any point of the continuum requiring nursing, medical or other care and attention. A great proportion of resources are used to service the repair and maintenance aspects of health care, despite policies towards promotion of health and prevention of disease. Health educators have a responsibility to see that the latter are progressively achieved, and to continue to urge for appropriate resource allocation as tools for reaching the stated goals.

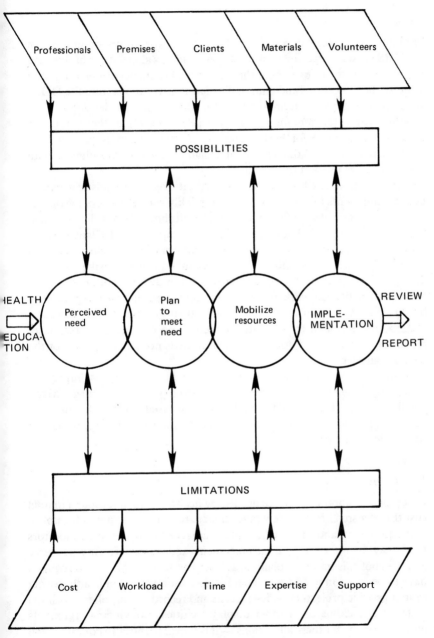

Figure 5   Programme planning, resource allocation

Premises

Premises are one facet of resources. The capital expenditure programme of the NHS shows staggering sums spent on buildings alone. Most of these are hospital premises to overcome the legacy of the nineteenth century, but some are health centres and clinics. The latest instructions from the DHSS about planning and building of premises do permit the development of facilities within the community. They urge, for example, that within the building programme for health centres, adequate space is provided for teaching purposes and that each centre plan is based on consultation with the prospective users of the premises.

Within a climate of low economic growth, it may be unrealistic to expect new developments to happen quickly, or quickly enough to be of maximum use — after all the year 2000 when health for all should be a reality — is just round the corner. It should be possible to improve and adapt existing premises to make them usable, and create the sort of environment required for effective health teaching. Many health educators 'make do', but documented reports to the right quarter, with indications of possible cost and cost-benefit, can work wonders. It is suggested that such reports may be unsolicited, sent in duplicate to more than one tier of the allocation system, and repeated at intervals. If there is no or a negative response, repetition and a revised approach are indicated, not an acceptance of the negative answers.

Although new or adapted premises may be one way of improving resources, some existing premises can be used to greater advantage. Many health centres, clinics and hospitals are underused for health-education purposes, full use of existing provision would lend weight to suggestions for additional resources.

Equipment

Equipment is another resource needed by health educators, though in total cost this is a small factor. Few practitioners have made requests for up-to-date equipment, and when such requests are received by resource allocators they may be greeted with astonishment and disbelief. Any resource allocation of this nature is planned at least 1 year in advance, and requests have to be made in good time. There is no reason why each health district cannot provide projectors, video screens and recorders, supplies of printed materials, blackboards or other display facilities. Convincing arguments have to be made for these allocations — it is hoped that health educators will realize their role and responsibility in arguing for appropriate equipment. Requests are often ignored because they seem insignificant compared with the demands for sophisticated machinery used in high-technology treatments, and because they seem so 'ordinary' compared with the demands of acute medicine and nursing. Requests for equipment have to be made strongly, firmly and clearly.

It is, however, essential to prove that any equipment provided would be used fully and expertly by more than one user. In some instances equipment has been provided and is then found to be underused or misused. Many authorities provide facilities to learn the use of machinery and equipment, and allow staff access to manuals of instruction or the manufacturer's demonstration sessions. Some authorities provide technical assistance in the use of equipment. This is helpful, but professionals still need to be aware of the possible uses they can make of equipment, and the correct application and maintenance procedures.

Printed materials may also be underused. Many authority headquarters have cupboards full of unused literature. There are two ways of overcoming this: one to make full use of whatever is available and ensure that a system is evolved of knowing what provision exists; the other to state quite clearly why certain material may not be appropriate for use, alerting the resource allocators to publications which would not enhance health-education efforts.

Management support

Management support and other support staffs are essential for practitioners to achieve maximum potential. The management structure of the NHS has undergone frequent modification. The principle is established whereby staff, including health educators, can expect management support for their efforts, whoever the manager of the future will be. Support is a two-way process, the managers can only support if they are made aware of the areas of practice which require assistance, and support can only be effective if it is accepted in a constructive manner. The level and volume of support will vary in each area, and should have the ultimate aim of greater self-sufficiency among practitioners. Managers do have the responsibility to account for staff activities and time, and thereby exercise a controlling function. Independent practice of each professional is bounded by the terms of employment, as well as the role and functions they have agreed to fulfil. It is, however, only the professional practitioner who can decide and communicate the decision on how practice could be improved.

Technical support

The quality and quantity of technical support services is likely to remain variable. Each authority within the NHS has library facilities and written material available to its practitioners although these are often underused. Many authorities provide libraries or similar facilities in schools of nursing or other centres. As this is a facility for all staff, full use of it should be made by ensuring that the content of the library is appropriate for all professional needs, that there is access at relevant times and that the facilities, when available, are actually used.

All health authorities regularly receive documents from government and other central agencies. This information should be available to all staff. Some authorities alert all staff to information received, others select the information they circulate. In each instance it is the professionals' responsibility to know where the information is stored, and how to gain access to it when required. Many authorities and their managers have offered open access to a part of headquarter offices. In several instances it is reported that this facility has not been used at all, and in other instances it is greatly underused. Geography and workload may make it difficult for each practitioner to use these facilities, but teamwork would ensure that one member of the team uses available opportunities, and takes responsibility for communication with colleagues and other team members. Many health districts are considering the use of computers for easy access to information. Such services as Prestel are already available. Practitioners need to familiarize themselves with the new technologies to gain their benefits.

Health authorities have established *health-education departments* in areas and districts. Whatever the strengths or limitations of individual departments, they do provide a focus for resources and a repository of knowledge about other possible resources, a stimulus for progressive action. Health-education departments should be able to provide an overview of activity in the area, and assist in a team approach to health education.

Central government departments, such as the DHSS, Welsh Office and Scottish Home and Health Department, could be regarded as a resource for practitioners. They provide information, training for professionals through the National Staff Committee and are active in monitoring local resource allocation within the NHS. Regional officers visit the service areas of the NHS and should be aware of available resources. The policy of government for prevention of disease and promotion of health could be used as a resource for increased provision and action.

Resources within local authorities

Professional practitioners within local authorities, such as teachers, social workers, environmental-health officers and architects, form one of the largest resources for health education with their variety of settings. The skills and expertise they bring to the task will vary, as will the level at which they are able to make an active contribution. The resource they provide within themselves is complemented by their support of efforts within the health services, and their contribution to the work of health-care teams.

Many local authorities have a direct input to health-education activities through their joint funding arrangements for special projects. Many of the established projects seek to meet proven needs, one aspect of which is health education, or rather education for healthy living. Few authorities can make a direct contribution to health education, except through the efforts of their component staffs. However, they do offer premises, equipment and utilization of resources which already exist, and encourage the linkage between health- and social-care teams.

Premises within local authorities range from ancient to modern, from specially designed for specific purposes to those inherited and difficult to maintain. This variety carries with it all the problems of heating, lighting and adaptation for specific use. However, it does give the opportunity to choose from a range of available possibilities. Health educators need to be aware of the availability of suitable premises, and use initiative in their utilization.

Educational establishments

Schools, colleges and higher-education establishments all come under the jurisdiction or influence of local authorities. They each have specific uses, but many have 'slack' periods, which could be used for health education. The health-education component of school curricula falls within the normal range of school premise use. Each school should have facilities for medical and nursing examinations, as well as first-aid resources. In reality there has often been a misuse of this agreed provision. The reasons for the varied usage of what should be ideal facilities for health education are many, but there seems no reason for continuing to accept poor or inadequate facilities. The minimum requirement for adequate health-care and health-education provisions appear to be a room, with right of access by health-care staff. The room should be of adequate size, sound proofing and lighting to carry out developmental assessments. Each room should also have storage facilities for equipment, and limited usage for other activities. Such provision is implicit in the Education Acts, it is becoming imperative with the implementation of the 1981 Act, and it is already available to health-care staffs working in schools in EEC countries. Out of 15 schools visited in various parts of France, and an equal number in Germany, only one had inadequate provision for health care, which was being rectified. Such rooms could then be used for health education, health counselling and routine procedures. The reality of inadequate provision is partly the responsibility of the local education authority, partly the result of acceptance by professional workers. School populations are at their lowest at present, therefore plans for schools can reasonably incorporate meeting the official commitments of authorities and the requirements of health-care workers.

School premises are underused for some part of the day and year. In theory, education authorities would welcome an extension of their use, but in practice there are some difficulties, such as the working hours and payment of caretaking personnel. Health educators should consider how they could make use of this facility, and the arrangements required to do so.

Colleges and establishments of further and higher education do not have a requirement to provide health-education facilities, except for the provision of first-aid and such measures as may fall within the Health and Safety at Work Act. However, many colleges are recognizing the needs of their students and are making facilities available. This is likely to increase with the implementation of youth training schemes, which will result in an influx of very young students. Many colleges hold summer schools and short courses, but it is noticeable that health education does not feature large in the curricula for these.

Some colleges and universities have student health services or pastoral services within their official structures. When these are linked to the services of community personnel, their impact and success is likely to increase.

Clubs

Clubs abound in many local authorities, serving a variety of groups with a variety of needs, from the very young to the very old, from those in need of help and treatment, to those who require shelter, warmth or company. The clubs and premises could be useful to health educators. Each local authority has different provision and policies, but very few do not have some such facility. In many places new sports and leisure centres provide a focus for the local community, and this could become an additional focus for health teaching and learning.

Materials

It requires some ingenuity to discover who has what materials available, who is responsible for their use and what conditions are attached to lending or borrowing them in local authorities. Usually this ingenuity pays dividends and the range of resources available for health education can increase manifold. An incidental by-product of such mutual aid is usually the establishment of contacts and personal relationships which are useful in many aspects of professional work.

Resources within voluntary agencies and societies

Each community has a variety of agencies and societies, each with a specific interest. Some, such as the Women's Royal Voluntary Service, contribute actively to health care within their community, others serve one aspect of health, and the majority have a vast reserve of capable and enthusiastic members of the public. The fact that people belong to clubs or societies shows that they are interested in a range of activities, however biased or subject specific the interests may be. Some clubs have fund-raising as their major activity, funds usually channelled to a particular community need. There is no reason to suppose that increased health-education activity could not be considered a particular need, or that some of these funds could not be used for health-education purposes. One example, Soroptimist International, an organization of professional and business women, is active in some 50 branches throughout the United Kingdom. They contribute funds for many local efforts to improve social and living conditions. Generally, they are alerted to acute needs, but it should be possible for a health educator to convince the local branch of the value of health, and the contribution of health education.

Apart from financial or material support by voluntary agencies, their members could become part of a health-education team, participating in the planning and evaluation parts of the process, and selectively contributing to subsequent actions. A resource of vast dimensions could be created, which would also serve to increase health awareness in that community; club and society members are also members of the community with networks of family, friends and acquaintances.

Commercial resources

There has been some reluctance by health-care personnel to utilize resources available through commercial or industrial channels. This stems from a suspicion of some sales techniques, and the traditional view that commercialism is 'not quite nice'. Sales techniques could provide the greatest resource for health educators, if they learn to use them appropriately. Health education is the business of selling health.

Commercial and industrial businesses do have a genuine concern for the well-being of their employees, often for such reasons as continuity of production and less risk of accidents. This concern can form the background to resource provision. Some businesses employ occupational health staff as resource people, others support the efforts made to create improved health within the community. Recently a number of industrial concerns have provided on-site facilities for pre-natal care and education for their female employees. Others have linked with such organisations as the Alcohol Education Council in an effort to reduce alcohol abuse. Through the years many firms have allowed access by arrangement and request for health education, preventive measures, such as inoculation, immunisation, and specific aspects of health care. In each of these instances, the resource provided by the workplace had to be sought and developed by the health educator.

Some commercial firms offer to make financial contribution to extend professional learning, and thereby resources and expertise. Others offer to contribute sums for specific purposes. The suspicion mentioned earlier is not usually realistic, and assurance can be obtained that commercial support is not product-specific, or affects the philosophy or intent of health education.

Some product-specific companies produce health education materials, e.g., anatomical atlases, which are extremely helpful and add to the resources available for practice.

Resources available through bodies with health-education functions

There are two national bodies whose sole purpose is the furtherance of health education, the Health Education Council and the Scottish Health Education Group. They are independent organizations, working within the framework of government directives and exchequer financial allocation. They have assisted in establishing health education as a concept to be considered in many ways. They have been active in the provision and encouragement of professional education and development, and in the international elements relating to health-education practice. They also provide a range of literature for use by public and practitioners, and produce regular information bulletins and resource lists. They are a resource for health educators in developing their practice, as well as a resource for government and other policy-making bodies in communicating needs and making demands at national levels.

Several other organizations have health education as their major function, each in a very different way, including:

1. BLAT — the education section of the British Life Assurance Trust, and therefore based on the commercial principles of insurance provision, modified by the Trust, which requires it to concentrate on providing teaching materials which will assist in improving health. BLAT have produced a range of health-education materials, used throughout the English-speaking world, the most recent being a package for education about cancers. They have been long established, but least active in Britain. They also vet materials produced by other organizations and give them a value rating. This rating is used extensively by overseas countries who wish to borrow or purchase health-education materials, and is valued by producers of materials in this country.

2. Family Planning Association provides a range of educational literature relevant to family life and family planning. They have pioneered educational methods related to the practice of family planning. They were so successful that their teaching has become part of health-service practice and incorporated in health education. They are now pioneering aspects of professional education, especially in the field of interpersonal relationships.

3. National Association of Maternal and Child Welfare provides a range of literature relevant to child development. They developed health clinics, which became incorporated into the National Health Service, and have been active in parentcraft and child-development education in schools and colleges since 1907.

Discussion of availability and use of resources could be extended, but each health educator will have to discover the resources most useful to his activity, use his initiative in obtaining them and extract the greatest possible value from each resource. The most wide-spread resource will always be people, and their individual and collective contribution. The discovery of resources and their use is an exercise in problem solving (Figure 6), a daily activity for most health workers, and one which constantly changes its

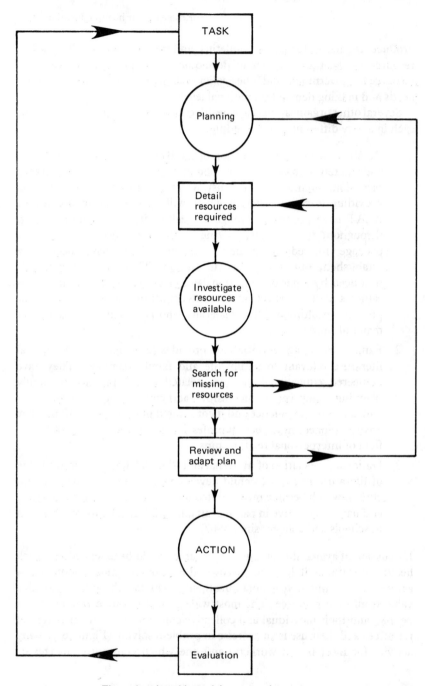

Figure 6   A problem solving approach to resources

dimensions and demands new inputs at each phase of the exercise. The conscious use of a problem-solving approach, or a process approach, will pay the greatest dividends.

Further reading

Brown, R G S (1973) The Changing Health Service, Routledge & Kegan Paul
DHSS (1978/79) Building Notes, HMSO

Useful addresses for additional resources or resource lists

National Association of Maternal and Child Welfare, 1 South Audley Street, London W1
Family Planning Association, Margaret Pyke House, Mortimer Street, London W1
Health Education Council, 78 New Oxford Street, London WC1A 1AH
Scottish Health Education Group, Woodburn House, Canaan Lane, Edinburgh EH10 4S6

CHAPTER 12

HEALTH EDUCATION FOR THE HEALTH EDUCATOR

God and the doctor we alike adore
But only when in danger, not before
The danger o'er, both are alike requited
God is forgotten and the doctor slighted.

Traditional saying, origin unknown

Health educators are neither gods nor, usually, doctors as mentioned above, but the principle appears to hold true. Health education and its practitioners appear to be wanted and adored for the wrong reasons, and when things look comparatively rosy, they are forgotten or feel slighted. Few policies, international, national or local, appear to include consideration of the needs of health educators as a group, nor is there reason to believe that they fare better as individuals. Some do have the backing of their professional group, and receive the same consideration and support as their professional group, others function in relative isolation. The following points apply to health-education practitioners, but they could apply equally to members of other groups of health workers. While the needs of the professional who functions as health educator are stressed, most points also apply to nonprofessional colleagues.

Stress and frustration

Everybody is subjected to the stresses of modern life. It seems that the stresses are escalating, and in turn creating further stress for professionals and their clients, which affects the practice of all health-related activity. The stresses inherent in modern life lead to increased need and demand for professional support and services and stretch the existing provision beyond realistic limits. In the end this turns full circle on itself. There may be external elements which can alleviate stress and frustrations, but in the first instance it will be the professional's self-help processes which will recognize when limits of tolerance are approaching, and when external resources will have to be sought. Everybody has an upper limit of tolerance, only the individual can know when the limit is reached and when scarce reserves are being drawn upon.

There is a positive side to stress — a certain amount of stress is normal and helps in being alert and active. Stress can be stimulating, and the limits mentioned above are elastic and can stretch to accommodate many situations. Stress can lead to creative thinking, to finding new ways of dealing with an otherwise intractable problem.

The range of stresses is as wide as health education itself. Stress may become dangerous when too many stress factors combine and create distortion, leading to malfunction. It is impossible to make an accurate prediction when the point of malfunction is reached, as it varies so much with individuals; awareness of the possibility is the only effective guard.

Personal problems affect the ability to function at the expected level. Many professionals have very high expectations of themselves, and often set unrealistic goals. It is wise to review these periodically and set realistic working targets, which meet the standards required of professional practitioners, but which take account of other factors. If it becomes apparent that professional standards or targets cannot be achieved, it is time to seek outside intervention, or make decisions on how to overcome the situation. Such review, or self-audit, forms a necessary part of professional practice. It is preferable to be one's own reviewer than having reviews superimposed, which can happen if malfunction becomes overt. Many employers use a form of annual review, based on self-audit in the first instance. This should enable personal and professional development, and assist in reducing some stress factors. Its use is relatively new to many practitioners, and can sometimes create a new form of stress.

It is stressful to work in a situation which is as fluid and constantly changing as health services are at present. There are always unknowns which have to be accepted in the planning processes and caring; there are uncertainties in general and particular terms, and there are all the contributory factors of increasing knowledge bases, increasing demands, increasing scope and decreasing or diminishing resources and returns. The returns are diminishing because the same factors are affecting everybody, and, therefore, they too are attempting to cope with them. This particular stress factor would have been considered important some years ago, it is now part of normal professional life, and one of the coping mechanisms developed is to accept it and automatically include it in planning and performing one's work.

Change in the working situation is usually compounded by rapid and frequent changes in the working environment, staff mobility, staff morbidity, changing roles and functions, changes in the management structure, etc. It requires special coping mechanisms to adapt to frequent changes. Most people are in the process of adaptation, and the process may be achieved more or less successfully. Time assists the process to occur naturally, but time is not always available — another stress factor.

There are two important side-effects of the processes described. The first is that processes of communication between management and staff become disrupted, and lines of communication have to be redrawn. It is important to keep an awareness of the current position, and if necessary to reconnect the essential communication networks. It is possible to keep an adequate information flow, in both directions, though constant vigilance is required. Communications between colleagues, in and outside the immediate professional circle, may also become more difficult and time-consuming; avoidance of communication breakdown is essential for reduction and resolution of this stress factor. The second side-effect is the possibility that some colleagues may function less efficiently when stress reaches a certain level. There has to be a dividing line between providing peer support and covering a potentially dangerous situation. Peer support contains an element of protection, which can be applied in situations of temporary imbalance, whether it is physical, mental or emotional. Peer support should not condone or collude with dangerous or potentially dangerous practices. The line is best drawn in consultation with colleagues and managers, and clearly communicated among all whom it might affect.

Another stress factor among many professionals is the need for accountability or audit, which are often regarded as threats. Self-audit should be part of professional practice, and while mildly stressful and requiring concentration and time, it need not develop into a major stress or strain. External audit has connotations of interference and control. If the audit is regarded as part of accountability it becomes less stressful. Accountability is part of life, and has to be accepted as part of any practice. It is possible to agree the mechanisms of accountability and audit by consultation and negotiations, and thereby reduce the stress factor. The factor will then remain as a stimulant to efficient practice, and to turning both accountability and audit into mechanisms for achieving improved resources and conditions and minimal control by outsiders.

The frustrations, which are also part of everyday life, but which can turn into stress factors, are consciousness of unmet needs, high workloads and insufficient resources to achieve set goals. Recognition of frustrations and plans to overcome them, even if the plans are long term, often reduce inherent stress.

Health care is a predominantly female profession, with the exception of medical consultants and some specialties. One real frustration is the multiplicity of roles and responsibilities expected of many female practitioners. We live in a society where women are responsible for home and family; at the same time the professional woman may be breadwinner, life-support system, caring daughter of elderly parents and professional practitioner. Although there have been changes in society leading to a reduction in this stress factor, it is likely to be with us for some time. Some practitioners feel frustrated at the double standard. Health education seeks to give women the choice to make decisions; life limits the choices available.

Last, but not least, there is considerable frustration when a professional's health suffers. Health educators, and health workers generally, are notorious for neglecting their own health needs, and seeking medical and other advice only at a late stage. Medical and other professionals incline to accept this undervaluation, and are reluctant to provide for the health care needs of the carers. One role for health educators of the future is to educate themselves into a realistic approach to their own health needs, and convince relevant professionals of the importance of health care for the carers.

Most people have built a range of coping mechanisms. For some it is immediate relief provided by shouting or going for a long, rapid walk, for others it takes a distancing from the situation and the facility to discuss the factors. Sometimes coping mechanisms become so much a part of the person that they are not recognized for what they are. These mechanisms form an essential safety valve, and should only be changed if better mechanisms are found.

There appears to be a fundamental belief that people are in professional practice, because they are able to cope with all the demands, stresses and frustrations of professional life. This is an oversimplification, but it does seem that most professionals have acquired, through their training, career and belonging to a defined group, strengths which allow coping mechanisms to operate and which are very flexible. It could be that pride in the profession and its aims and objectives override any personal concerns. It is not clear where the limitations are, and how far professionalism and goodwill can be stretched.

Everybody, and especially people working in stressful situations, needs to relax. Professional practice often implies that stated working hours do not represent the actual hours worked. The need for leisure becomes more vital. Each individual should choose the most suitable method of relaxation; it could be a few hours of doing nothing at all, activity to keep their bodies in trim, art or drama, socializing with people outside the professional's work. Some people have found relaxation is enhanced by the practice of yoga or meditation, others by reading material unrelated to work. Those who feel that a professional has no right to relax call it escapism, but others consider it an essential element of being able to cope with the stresses mentioned, and to enable the person to develop personally and professionally. The latter view seems more realistic, as it stimulates new approaches to the everyday range of activities and stresses.

It is recognized by most professionals that they cannot function effectively in isolation. Each professional group should, therefore, build support systems to lessen stress by sharing experiences and concerns. Support systems can range widely, for example, peer, management, extra-professional, family, counselling, co-counselling are systems in current use. It is advisable to find the system or systems which serve the purpose best in the shortest possible time. It is important, however, to build the systems before a crisis is reached, so that they are available when needed.

Other factors

New recruits require additional support to become experts at health education. Every professional has a responsibility to assist in the induction of newcomers. The induction may be no more than demonstrating availability and approachability, or willingness to discuss and support if necessary. This can be very comforting, and lessen the additional stress of being new and unfamiliar with colleagues and facilities. It may also require uncritical acceptance of new ideas and, as a result, a modification of one's own ideas and practice. The importance of evaluation for newcomers cannot be stressed enough, it is very disheartening if success is not as obvious as expected, and the expert can bring balance to smaller, but very real, achievements. Most newcomers will have had some professional training, although it may not be the same background as that of the experienced practitioner. Mutual benefit can be gained by learning from each other, newness should not inhibit the exchange of information and ideas.

Theories of health education are few, and none are proven. Application of theories of learning, motivation, education and health all have their place. In general, health education has to be seen as a very practical skill, drawing on available theories to enhance practice, but extracting relevant parts and adapting them to the practical situations. It is possible that eventually a theory of health education will emerge. There is a suspicion that a theory of health education could actually inhibit practice, and make it less all embracing and useful.

Knowledge is an essential prerequisite for being a health educator, and with this the facility to enhance existing, acquire new and reject out-dated knowledge. The essentials for health education are to remain receptive to new ideas and to develop critical faculties so that newly available information, whether research-based or disseminated by other means, can be considered for its relevance, usefulness and validity. Acquisition of knowledge is a two-way process, and the health educator has many opportunities to learn from the client groups as well as through official channels.

There is some feeling that health educators should 'be ahead' of the client and target groups in their knowledge and skills. This seems nonsense if the principle of a partnership approach is valid. Health educators should be knowledgeable about health matters, related matters may be equally well taught by other group members. As a professional the health educator should be able to acknowledge matters outside the relevant expertise, and that there is not only willingness to learn about them, but interest and eagerness.

Personal example

The question of being an exemplar is considered in Chapter 7. As a resource person the health educator has needs. First, and most important, there is the need to be oneself, not always to wear the mantle of 'professional'. Personal qualities and personality can bring much to health education, and in return the health educator will receive a natural response from clients. The establishment of interpersonal relationships at all levels will be eased by being natural. Pretence can easily turn into pretentiousness and create barriers of communications. Some people may feel that there are facets to their character which they do not wish to reveal to client groups, but this has to be a personal decision. Some people may feel that their 'natural' character may prove unacceptable, they are likely to be surprised how tolerant people are, and how much they welcome personal differences.

Professionals, especially nurses, cannot help being influential. There is an acceptance within the general public that 'nurses should know', often based on unrealistic expectations and stereotyping. This position has to be accepted occasionally, and efforts made to meet expectations. Awareness of influence should lead to using it with due care and beneficial effect. Personal example is another matter. There may be certain personal standards to meet, inherent in being a health educator, such as cleanliness and a reasonably tidy appearance.

Health educators cannot be expected to meet all the health targets set. They may be over- or underweight, they may be smokers, or they may not take kindly to physical exercise. They have to accept, however, that their role requires them, in personal and professional life, to be seen to be moderate in most things, to indulge in nonhealth activities with caution and to keep all their behaviours within the bounds of professional practice.

Further reading

Hilgard, E and Atkinson, R Introduction to Psychology, 7th edition, Harcourt Brace Jovanovich
Smith, P (1980) Group Processes and Personal Change, Harper & Row

CHAPTER 13

TRENDS IN HEALTH EDUCATION

Health education is one of the most important aspects of preventive medicine.

DHSS (1977) White Paper 'Prevention and Health' HMSO

In an unpublished address to senior nurse managers, Dr Maryon Davies (HEC) in 1975, upon the first reorganization of the National Health Service, described the ultimate in health education. He outlined how health could be achieved by enforced legislation, making behaviour which leads to ill-health or severe risk of illness punishable in law, and excluding anyone suffering from self-inflicted disease from society. The message was very clear — health education is required on many levels to avoid any totalitarian or desperate approach becoming reality.

It is not easy to talk about trends within such a vast subject area, as the current climate or trend changes so rapidly.

General knowledge

The most fundamental and pervasive change which appears to represent a continuing trend relates to the level of general knowledge within the general public. Everyone has opinions about health matters, and each person believes they know best.

Fundamental beliefs and attitudes are handed down from generation to generation. Young people are said to believe and act contrary to established mores, but most of the shifts in beliefs and attitudes are slight. As young people get older their heritage manifests itself. Therefore, trends, as they apply to individuals, may be age related — young people expressing their opinions loudly, but based on little solid foundation and older people holding firmly rooted convictions which find less vocal expression. The sum total of trends will therefore remain an unknown factor, considering the multitude of persons, small groups and the range of subjects health education encompasses. The following points are based on more discernible trends, such as stated policies at various levels, fashions and conflict, language and changing meanings of words and the impact of minority groups upon society.

Government policies

Government policies may conflict directly, as demonstrated in the support of health education and prevention by the DHSS and the contrary actions of the Treasury. There is a very genuine desire to eliminate and eradicate disease and to lessen self-inflicted trauma, such as that caused by addictions of all sorts or avoidable accidents, to curtail by these means cost and demands on acute medical and allied services.

Government resources

The drain on government resources caused by the payment of sickness benefit or allowances to disabled persons is constantly escalating. This has to be calculated in the context of a dwindling workforce, who are direct contributors to funds from which benefits and resources are drawn. The complexity of this is compounded, as the reduction in workforce is due to a variety of causes, the ageing population, fewer children, rising unemployment, rising part-time occupations which do not require state insurance contributions, and rising female employment where contribution on a full scale may be optional. However, there is income received by the Exchequer from the production and distribution of harmful substances, such as tobacco, alcohol, petrol with high lead content. In any statistics and public accounts the income from the above sources and others exceeds expenditure on health and health education, but forms part of the general purse from which all benefits are paid.

One recent source of government income has been the levy on betting and other forms of gambling, which has been described by some as a national disease, and is certainly a cause of social breakdown, leading to ill-health of family members. Gambling is one of the addictions which is stretching health and social services provision in some areas of the country.

Another increasing source of government income, and at the same time an increasing cause of debility or overt ill-health, is the expansion in the range of proprietary drugs and foods. Many proprietary foods contain harmful substances. The government requires that the food content is described on labels or packaging materials, but neither the checks on accuracy of labelling nor their readability or comprehensiveness are adequate.

It has been shown that most medicines can cause harm, yet bottles and packs freely available from chemist shops and supermarkets do not tell the customer about possible side-effects or clearly describe the safe upper limit of consuming such preparations. There is a review body which makes recommendations on the safety of drugs to the government of the day. The advice of the review body is followed where substantive evidence of harm exists, or where pressure to act has been too strong to be ignored. Marketing of any substance is possible, pending patent or acceptance by government organizations, as long as the small print on the package states 'patent applied for'. It has been shown, mainly by responsible reporting within the mass media, that government action often is too little and too late. Health educators may have to increase their contribution, at every level and by all means, in emphasizing the hazards of some products, the safe use of prescribed drugs and add to the pressures to make product labelling, including foods and drugs, more comprehensive and readable.

First official interest in health education was manifest in 1964, when the Cohen Committee on Health Education reported. This provided the stimulus for development of health education within the National Health and Personal Social Services. This impetus has been maintained spasmodically. However, some of the recommendations made in 1964, and accepted in principle by the government of the day, have yet to be implemented, and still constitute targets for achievement.

Since 1948, when the National Health Service came into being, preventive measures have been part of statutory provision, theoretically available freely to all. Preventive actions are not easy to quantify, or prove qualitatively, and no objective assessment or proof of need has been available. Therefore they have remained the Cinderella elements of the total service, with heavy commitment of staff and other resources towards sickness and repair. The major demands exist in treatment and repair services, such as surgery, and recently the development of transplant surgery and other high-cost, high-technology techniques. The ethical implications of such allocation are subject to public debate at present, and they are too vast and far reaching to be adequately reflected here.

Prevention

There have been signs that successive governments are realizing that prevention, and health eduation as a means of prevention, should play a distinct role. During the past 5–6 years several documents, which are designed to stimulate preventive action, have been published by government departments: 'Prevention and Health' (1976) was the first of a series, 'Alcohol in the Work-place' (1981) is the latest. All of these show a clear trend towards an emphasis on health, but this is not fully supported by appropriate follow-up action, including adequate resource allocation. Taken overall, governmental support of health and health education remains comparatively low. However, several government departments have been involved in the production of relevant documents, and trends towards prevention are apparent. A few examples follow.

1. The DHSS has persuaded cigarette manufacturers to print a health warning on cigarette packets in an attempt to alert the public to the dangers of smoking. It is arguable whether the printing of cigarette packets has made them more attractive and whether confirmed smokers ignore the actual words.

2. Various sections of government have been involved in negotiations with advertisers, and voluntary codes of practice have been agreed. Some advertising is restricted to adult access, direct advertising of alcohol and tobacco on television has become unacceptable, and all advertisements should follow the agreed codes. This in no way inhibits indirect advertising, and has encouraged more imaginative use of available outlets.

3. DHSS and Exchequer funding of the Health Education Concil and the Scottish Health Education Group has enabled concentration of effort and stimulated a range of activities, including continuing education for professionals and support of health-education officers.

4. The DES established a Schools Council some years ago. The Schools and Health Education Councils, as a partnership, have developed teaching and learning packages specific to health-education programmes in schools. The packages have been tried and tested, and are arranged for various age groups. They are useful aids to many teachers and are a joy to those pupils who have access to them. The dissemination of this material was not easy, and its availability in schools throughout England is still variable. Presently the role of the Schools Council is being reconsidered and it is to be hoped that the successes of the past will not be lost.

5. Scotland has a government-funded Health Education Group which has produced some very attractive materials informing the public about health matters and giving professional tools for more effective health education. They also contribute to the further education of professional practitioners in health education.

6. The greatest impact from the DES has been in teacher training. A health-education option is now available to many trainee teachers. As they qualify and take up teaching posts, the progress of health education in schools should be enhanced. There have also been short courses for teachers, and inservice training programmes to assist them in developing their skills in teaching health subjects and related syllabuses, such as child care.

7. The Health and Safety Executive, established as a result of the Health and Safety at Work Act 1973 has stimulated health education activity in industry, commerce and educational establishments. There is concern that present economic pressures are having a detrimental and serious effect on the Executive's effectiveness.

8. Legislation introduced in January 1983 made wearing seat belts in cars compulsory. This is an attempt to reduce the effects of accidents, and is the outcome of much public pressure.

9. There is a range of legislation which has been a response, however delayed and inadequately applied or enforced, to health educators' expressed concern, for example, regulating sale of fireworks to children, lead content of toys and paints, use of distinctive receptacles for poisonous substances. The major problem is that no legislation can respond to newly discovered health hazards sufficiently quickly nor can it ever be applied with total effect whilst living in a democratic society.

Local government services

Local government departments have varied responsibilities, some of which are subject to legislation applicable throughout the United Kingdom, others subject to regional variations and still others affected by by-laws. The boundaries of local authorities do not always follow logical patterns, and recent boundary changes have not served to lessen the confusion in every case.

The relative wealth or poverty of any local authority depends on several sources of revenue, and is therefore closely related to the constitution of its component parts. The plight of inner cities with their multiple problems and declining revenue is the best illustration of this. One source of revenue is government funding, which has varied according to the political philosophy of the times, the economic state of the country and the overall allocation of national resources. This in turn means that no local authority can be sure of the amount of money or other help it will receive in any one year, and it does not often bear any relation to the authorities' expressed needs or wishes, alters their proposed spending and makes long-term planning difficult.

The second source of funding is through domestic and commercial rates. At a time when industry is contracting and when commercial concerns are facing difficulty, the burden on some ratepayers is proportionately increased. Most authorities attempt to make allowances for those within their jurisdiction who have special needs. Authorities who have a large itinerant population, or old and poor housing, receive proportionately less revenue from this source, thus making improvements in environmental conditions even more difficult.

The third source of revenue is for services rendered, such as planning applications, copies of documents, search fees when purchasing a house. This is a steady, but small source of revenue, which also contracts in times of economic stringency when people are reluctant to move house or to spend money on building extensions.

Each local authority employs staff to service the various departments at headquarters and to provide external services. Staffing policies vary, and establishments are affected by local and national conditions. The members of local authorities are elected, and may be in office for their personal qualities, their expertise or their political affiliation. Their term of office can be as short as 3 years or they may be re-elected. The overall policy of the authority is usually related to the political majority among its elected members. Changes in policy can be frequent, and long-term planning becomes difficult for many authorities.

The thumbnail sketch provided above is essential to understand the trends in health education within any authority, and the fact that although many services have a health-education component this may be a neglected aspect of the service. The departments mentioned below are selected for their overt health-education role. Many others, such as street cleansing and refuse collection, influence in other ways the health of the community served by any particular authority.

Social service departments

Social service departments have stated that they wish their workers to make every effort towards prevention of adverse conditions relating to the health of the family or community. This may manifest itself in active health-education programmes, but more usually is confined to the case/workload of practitioners. Trained and qualified social workers are familiar with human development, and have studied many aspects of human behaviour. Some social workers are reasonably expert at behaviour modification techniques, which could be used in health-education practice, others have expertise in dealing with specific groups.

The stated policy is that social work will move towards graduate entry, and that all social workers will be trained practitioners, though the level and format of professional preparation will vary. In practice there has been little change in the number of graduates employed during the past 10 years, and an average of 50% of social workers remain untrained, the same level as existed 10 years ago. At the same time the numbers of clients requiring social-work services, especially the elderly and families with unemployed members, or at risk of nonaccidental injury, are increasing. Local authorities have not increased establishments of social-work staff, and in some instances there has been a contraction of service. All this has led to the situation where professional social workers would welcome involvement in health education, but are often unable to contribute or participate.

On the positive side there are an increasing number of social workers who are members of a primary health-care team, or who have formed close liaison with members of the team, and whose contribution to health education is considerable.

Environmental-health officers

Environmental-health officers make a considerable contribution to health education, within the parameters of their role and functions. Their paramount concern is public health and safety, and the various Acts of Parliament relating to sale, consumption and storage of food form a large element of their work. The annual reports by the Chief Medical Officer contain accounts of the work of these officers. Recently, in some authorities, seminars led by environmental-health officers have been held for those in the food trade, in an attempt to affect public health through education rather than legislation. Some officers contribute to the learning of other professionals, others liaise in order to communicate discovered needs and to share in planning how to overcome these. Like everybody else working in local government services, staff establishments have not increased and any desire to participate in health-education programmes has to be limited by reality.

Schools and colleges

Schools and colleges come under the jurisdiction of local authorities. Health education in schools is discussed elsewhere but it is important to reiterate that the majority of teachers are aware that health education should form part of the curriculum. Some teachers are enthusiastic health educators, more teachers are able to study health education as part of their professional training and most would welcome a stronger role within the subject, but are constrained by their existing teaching loads.

There has been a national policy to curtail the number of people entering teacher training, and many local authority education commitees have introduced drastic cuts in the numbers of teachers they employ. The cuts have been documented in terms of pupil : teacher ratios, which have not improved to cope with special needs, and the birthrate as it was until 1977 or 1978, which led planners to believe that the fall in the school population would continue and that the requirements for teachers would drop. There is evidence that there was an increase in the birth-rate from 1977 onwards and that the increase will be maintained, though the rate of increase has reached a plateau. One effect of increasing unemployment is likely to be a further increase in birth-rate, not only because it is a traditional pattern of such difficulties, but because many people can no longer afford the cost of family-planning materials. The immediate effect on health education in schools is likely to be that teachers will be unable to extend the health education aspects of their work, despite their keenness and willingness to do so; they are likely to look to professional outsiders to a much greater extent. The long-term effect could be a need to increase input considerably.

The police

Police officers in most authorities are involved with the health of the community in many ways. Their most immediate and active contribution has to be in the case of disturbance of any kind, which often relates to breakdown of health. They often have to cope with the worst aspects of failure in health care, and are active participants in most instances of providing services for cases of nonaccidental injury. Most officers liaise with members of the primary health-care team, with hospitals and with schools, often on a regular basis but certainly when their expertise is required. Their major contribution to formal health education is in the fields of drug abuse and accident prevention. Their less formal contribution may range widely, especially as liaison members to youth clubs and organizers of other kinds of social activity.

Highways

Highways departments have a health function, in their responsibility for street lighting, etc. They do not often contribute to formal programmes of health education, but their informal input can be wide-ranging. They are the experts at communication by symbol and signal, and the development of easily recognizable symbols has far-reaching effects. Much research has been undertaken by these departments on communications and their greatest contribution could be by the publication of research and dissemination of research findings.

Facilities in local government

Facilities available in local authorities vary. Many of these could be useful for health education, such as premises, clubs, swimming pools, sports centres and rooms in town halls. Many authorities regret the limits of their active involvement in health education, and it has always been their policy to allow use of their facilities for professionals working in other contexts. This trend is still the intent of most authorities, but there have been practical difficulties, such as cost of heating and lighting, caretaking and maintenance, especially if premises are used at irregular hours. However, it is usually possible to make arrangements about the use of facilities.

Other agencies

Community-health councils

Community-health councils initially showed great interest in the maintenance of health and the preventive services. The interest is still current, but many councils are under a lot of pressure to improve acute facilities, and staff time has to be spent in handling complaints. Many councils make an active contribution to health education by information displays, and starting preventive programmes. Health educators could usefully avail themselves of the interest and support they might receive from their local community-health council. The government has been persuaded that the retention of this consumer voice is desirable, and the councils can therefore plan ahead.

Voluntary agencies

Voluntary agencies make a significant contribution to the health of any community, and also to health education. It is sometimes difficult to determine which agency can truly be called 'voluntary' as so many receive financial support from local or national governments. The least complex definition would be any agency which has its own constitution, rules and regulations and which does not depend on professional staff for its activities. In many instances health education forms part of the ambit of an agency. A few particular examples follow.

1. Special interest groups for a range of conditions are increasing. Usually the initial reason for the group's formation is to provide self-help for sufferers from specific, handicapping conditions. This soon changes into support for group members and their families. Arising out of self-help comes a mutual educative programme ranging through all life activities, including health. Very often the group develops into a pressure group to influence a particular aspect of service provision, or local or national policies. The educative function of the group relates to its own members, any prospective member, inquirers with similar interests and the general public. Some groups are critical of professional services, others welcome professional input. Health educators can usefully contact many of these groups, to offer their services and in turn they are likely to acquire new and additional knowledge and information.

2. The marriage-guidance councils have existed in their specific functions for many years. In the past decade they have developed their educative roles to a large extent, and some of their counsellors make a significant contribution to health education in schools, colleges, clinics, clubs and programmes of professional education and training.

3. The Family Planning Association initially provided a specific service, and researched methods of family planning and a range of possible supplies. The service aspect of their work has been incorporated into the National Health Service, with the exception of specialist input

such as male sterilization. The educative role has increased. The main thrust of education has been for practitioners in professional roles and in residential establishments. The major contribution has been in the range of education for improved interpersonal relationships.

4. Citizen's Advice Bureaux (CAB) play a role in educating the general public about availability and range of services. In many instances their contribution goes beyond the merely factual and consists of counselling and personal advice. Few CABs have evolved formal programmes of health education, but have been instrumental in highlighting needs and opportunities.

Trends in the National Health Service

Similar to local government services, all sections of the Health Service are subject to scrutiny in view of economic stringencies and resource allocation. The national allocation of financial resources since 1978 has sought to redress imbalance by distributing proportionately greater amounts to more deprived areas. In practical terms this has meant a shortage of ready money in the better-off areas, as they found that the needs and demands did not reduce in line with reduced income. The situation is made more complex by certain centres having greater and unequal demands related to specialist services, building programmes, technological developments and being recognized centres for people outside the immediate vicinity. Additionally, some centres provide education and training for a variety of health professionals. Some are totally reliant on state funding, others are in receipt of funds from trusts, investments, and special funds. The ideology behind the redistribution of resources may be acceptable, but at present it has highlighted problems and given rise to new dilemmas. All this is happening at a time of inflation, when wages and salaries are rising and when new instruments and technologies should be available. Some parts of the service are also facing greater demands, such as services for elderly people, preventive measures against nonaccidental injury and transplant surgery. The difficulties encountered in decisionmaking are enormous. Often there are pressures arising from special interest groups and professional groups, such as consultants, with special expertise. Political pressures can also influence decisions, and some groups within the Health Service are better organized politically than others.

Health educators, especially health professionals, are not known for their contribution to the political arena, but recently more have become active in local and national government. The trend should be to increase this interest and influence, not necessarily at party-political level, but throughout the policy- and decisionmaking processes.

The DHSS have clearly declared their interest and support of preventive measures, and officially this should be interpreted as an adequate allocation of resources to be able to implement prevention, employ staff to do so and use all available expertise in this direction. In practice the trend is not all that clear, and health educators may have the task of educating the decisionmakers, or drawing public attention to obvious disadvantages.

Some of the government support for prevention has been specifically geared towards priority groups, such as schoolchildren and alcoholics. At present the government is considering a full-scale inquiry into the role and functions of health visitors and school nurses, which is likely to demonstrate the need to implement their previous recommendations, and define realistic case/workloads.

Most people working in the public-health field, or in hospital departments most closely allied to public health, are finding that their functions are increasing, the volume and nature of their work is leading to additional load and there are many aspects which are in need of attention which they are unable to provide. The main reason why there is undermanning in public-health areas is lack of people with the qualifications and experience to carry out the work. Establishments have not increased overall for many years, and in some parts of the country agreed establishments have not been filled. The reason given is 'shortage of money', but this is only part of the story. Whilst the trend has been stated by government, it has yet to be followed by the employing authorities within the Health Service.

In 1974 each health authority was enabled to establish a health-education section or department, but some failed to do so. This was seen as a sign that health education was finally being given official recognition and the facility for development. In 1982 the Health Service was restructured and the future of health-education departments is again uncertain.

In 1981, as a direct result of the report on Children with Special Needs (Warnock), an Education Act was passed, which is likely to have as much impact on health as education services. It requires professional nursing input into all schools, at a level which is presently possible only in very few areas, and expertise and skill in writing and collating of reports, and communicating with parents, which is unparalleled in the past.

Most official changes within the National Health Service in recent years should have benefited all component parts of prevention, but this has yet to become a reality.

Trade unions

Trade unions are involved in negotiations relating to conditions of service and pay structures for Health Service workers. The outcomes of such negotiations will affect the number of people attracted to work within the Health Service, and the structure will have implications for development of specific expertise and career progression, i.e., the number of people who remain working in the Health Service.

A constructive contribution to health education has been made by some trade unions. They have passed resolutions which support the intentions of health educators, and have applied pressures for measures which could lead to positive health. Some trade unions have active education programmes for their members, and in recent years part of this continuing education has included health education. Trade unions have also been instrumental in applying safety measures in work places, and creating facilities for health and education programmes to be carried out.

Professionalization

Many groups who contribute to health education are considered to be professional. There is still a divergence of opinion whether these groups gain or lose by professionalization. The traditional professions are being challenged, and they are no longer exclusive. Aspiring professionals may be better perceived as competent practitioners with a real contribution to caring for people than as members of professional groups whose impact is lessening and whose rights and privileges are being threatened and curtailed. Some of the traditional professions are surviving the threat by adapting their roles and public images, such as doctors, and it is noticeable that they have recently 'discovered' prevention. Many of them remain unaware that there are people who have been active in this area for many years and who already are able to provide the necessary skills and competences. Health educators of the future will play a large role in educating doctors if they are to gain proficiency in practising prevention and making a real contribution to health education.

Further reading

Brown, R G S (1973) The Changing National Health Service, Routledge & Kegan Paul

Garner, L (1979) The NHS—Your Money or Your Life, Penguin

Schools Council (1982) '13–18', Forbes Publications and TACADE

Government publications

(1964) Health Education, Report of the Joint Committee of the Central and Scottish Health Services Councils, Chairman Lord Cohen of Birkenhead, HMSO

(1976) Prevention and Health, Everybody's Business, a consultative document, HMSO

(1977) Prevention and Health, white paper, HMSO

(1977) Prevention and Health: Reducing the Risk — Safer Pregnancy and Childbirth, HMSO

(1978) Prevention and Health, Occupational Health Services — the Way Ahead, Discussion document by the Health and Safety Commission, HMSO

(1980) Towards Better Health Care for Schoolchildren in Scotland, SHHD/SED, HMSO

(1980) The Pattern and Range of Services for Problem Drinkers, Report by the Advisory Committee on Alcoholism, HMSO

(until 1974) On the State of the Public Health, annual reports of the Chief Medical Officer

CHAPTER 14

THE INTERNATIONAL CONTEXT

> All are architects of Fate,
> Working in these walls of Time;
> Some with massive deeds and great,
> Some with ornaments of rhyme.
>
> . . .
>
> Nothing useless is, or low;
> Each thing in its place is best;
> And what seems but idle show
> Strengthens and supports the rest.
>
> from 'The Builders', Longfellow

Internationally health education is being practised and developed in a vast variety of ways, by a variety of workers. In many instances health-education practice arises out of other established social, cultural or sports activities and becomes an integral part of that activity. Some people equate health with sport, to them health and fitness is synonymous. Others accept this premise, but feel that either health or sport is out of their reach, so making the task of the health educator more onerous.

The disadvantages of such wide variety are that no one person or organization can possibly be aware of the total picture, and that the variables for evaluation are too numerous to produce the sort of evidence of success required to satisfy all critics. Proof remains scanty or unacceptable in scientific terms or usable as a political or management tool. This lack of proof should be no barrier to progress, especially if one follows de Bono's maxim "Proof is just a lack of imagination — of alternatives" (de Bono, 1982). Advantages far outweigh disadvantages, and variety allows adaptation to local circumstances, full usage of individual skills and imaginative use of scarce resources. Policy makers and practitioners alike

161

fully recognize that health education has great potential and value, but a vestige of suspicion remains. The suspicion appears to be a fear of the unknown, and of not being able to control or inhibit events once they have got under way.

Conferences and journals

One manifestation of international interest is the organization of international conferences. The 10th International Conference on Health Education was held in London in 1979, previous venues having been in nine other countries. Speakers from all corners of the world presented papers; exhibitions and films from many countries demonstrated the range of possible efforts and shared those methods and practices which had proved to be successful and acceptable. Most importantly, representatives from 78 countries were able to meet and discuss the many facets of their work and explain their perceived needs and ideas. Each international conference receives follow-up by means of detailed reports. The report of the 10th conference provides worth-while and interesting reading (HEC, 1980). Unfortunately the reports are usually circulated only to participants and are not always drawn to the attention of others. Conferences and reports provide a forum for exchanging ideas and disseminating information, but there is a desire among practitioners to have more speedy access to the material produced, so that many more can improve their knowledge, techniques, practices and widen their horizons.

Another important international means of helping all those involved or interested in health education is the journal 'News Bulletin' published by the International Union for Health Education. This briefly reviews events, campaigns and programmes, research, training and reports on people involved in these activities throughout Europe and other countries. Reports from England, Wales or Scotland may be written in German or French, and reports from other parts of Europe may be in any of three languages. The problems and concerns are the same wherever one happens to be. Individual articles are sufficiently brief to understand the gist, if not all the words (News, 1982).

International developments

The progress of health education is taking very different paths in different countries.

Developed or industrial countries suffer the disadvantage that both health and education are competing with vested interests, such as insurance-based health finance for the USA and parts of Europe, or advertising and commerce, such as the tobacco and drinks industries. Developing countries can decide, and are generally encouraged to do so, on schemes and services which will benefit the greatest number of people. It would appear that if Europe, and within this the United Kingdom, could consider itself a developing not a developed country, health education would accelerate in all its dimensions and make great strides forward. It would be impossible to review all that is happening at present in the developed countries, but a few examples may give a reasonable indication.

The latest edition of 'Health Education in Europe' was published in 1980 and describes activities in 30 countries, among which England, Wales and Northern Ireland are considered separately from Scotland (Kaplun and Erben, 1980). In each description for each of the 30 countries, there appears to be a gap between the stated, desirable goals and practice, and the actual achievements. But in each instance some progress can be discerned. Most noticeable is that all countries have attempted to make messages contained in health-education materials and teaching programmes more attractive and relevant. Some, like Poland, have designated special periods of time annually so that reinforcement of teaching can easily occur, and to ensure that the depth of learning and teaching can be increased.

Europe

Some schemes seem to demonstrate the underlying philosophy of health education more clearly than others, such as creating independence through healthy living.

Example 1. Belgium. In selected Belgian schools, children not only receive the usual range of nursing and medical care, but are actively encouraged to participate in planning their health care, including their programme of health education. The child, parent, teacher and caring professional make an implicit contract to follow their part of the plan, and it is agreed at the planning stage who will take the responsibility for certain actions. This means that the school nurse or health visitor may teach the facts about nutrition, the class teacher will reinforce the health teaching, parents will endeavour to provide a balanced or otherwise recommended diet and the child will attempt to maintain the diet agreed, as well as learn the reasons why this may be necessary and how he/she can maintain their health when the agreed programme is completed. The school doctor continues his monitoring role in developmental terms, and the nurse and doctor assess progress using the established assessment procedures and maintaining detailed and accurate records. Those involved in the plan must be mutually compatible, and counselling skills may be required at phases throughout the programme.

Diet has been quoted in the example, and avoidance of obesity, but the idea can be used in any health-care area or with any age group. Preliminary results and evaluations show that the health-education advice and counselling which form part of the care plan are proving acceptable and that the success rate is high. Long-term evaluations are being carried out and, hopefully, will show the change in attitudes to health desired by most health educators. It will be of particular interest to discover whether in the very long term this type of programme will alter the need for professional input, or whether it provides sufficient stimulus for self-care throughout life. If it proves to be successful in the long term, it could portend changes immediate and far-reaching in professional practice.

Example 2. France.   The French equivalent of the DHSS declared school health and school nursing a priority some years ago. In each school nurse's job specification it is stated that she should spend approximately 50% of her working time practising health education. This has meant that this group of nurses have become very skilled practitioners, and they have been able to carry out their functions in the way considered most appropriate to the schools for which they carry responsibility. During 1981 I was seconded to observe the resulting practice, and a few of the ways and methods follow:

1. In some schools the nurse, or all the school nurses in a given district together with their nurse-manager, agrees the subjects to be taught during the term or year. This can consist of one topic of current relevance or a complicated programme. The selected topic and its component subjects are then taught by the nurse to every form within the school, wherever possible involving the class or subject teacher. The intent is to ensure that every pupil is in receipt of similar basic information, albeit at differing levels of knowledge and understanding. Teacher involvement ensures that the health specialists' teaching can be supported and reinforced. Providing health-education programmes in this way has been found more effective in informing parents than other ways directed at the adult population.

2. In many senior or comprehensive schools health clubs have been established. These have the same status as other general school activity clubs. They take place at the same time of the same day each week, and attendance is voluntary. The organization of each 'club de santé' varies, but two patterns appear to be most successful. In the first instance the school nurse decides a programme for a stated number of weeks and publicizes this throughout the school. Those interested pupils attend as they desire or as they have been advised by teachers and parents.

Alternatively the initial weeks of any school year are used to discover 'need' in terms of information and knowledge, by discussion with pupils and teachers or the use of a suggestion box. A programme is then evolved for and with the participant group. Doctors, teachers and other specialists may be invited to join particular sessions. The invitation is made by the nurse, and relies on her decision of professional competence, knowing whether and when additional expert input would be appropriate. Despite their voluntary nature the clubs appear to be well attended. I observed several in operation in the Haute-de-Seine Health District on the outskirts of Paris. Participation was active in all cases. In one club the clerical assistant joined the group, taking the point of view a parent would be likely to take. Numbers of pupils at any session varied from a mere handful to over 30. I was informed that actual membership of the club was approximately 70 pupils but attendance depended not only on the subject and the enthusiasm of the leader, but also on pressures from other parts of the school curriculum. A curve of attendance could be drawn, high through the winter months, dropping with the approach of examinations and hot weather lethargy.

3. In one middle school the agreed topic was dental hygiene, and general development of teeth. The nurse instructed three of the upper forms, and provided them with a range of equipment, from individual tooth-brushes to sets of model jaws and dentists tools. The older children then split into groups, each group prepared a project including drawings and posters which could be used as visual aids. They were able to use the nurse as a resource person if they needed help or had unanswered questions. When the projects were complete the groups toured all other classes in the school, and gave a demonstration and talk. Nurse and teachers were able to support with comments and in answering questions. The older children appeared to learn easily and

happily, the younger children enjoyed the produced visual material and also appeared to learn a substantial amount.

Example 3. Germany.   Germany has reason to be very concerned about the problems associated with the abuse of alcohol, both among its young and adult populations. The numbers of people being treated for alcoholism, an increase in alcohol-related diseases and the social and criminal effects of excess alcohol consumption are reaching epidemic proportions. Though Germany is used as an example, the same problem is acute in many countries. Education to counteract alcohol abuse is currently one of the major interests of the United Kingdom's health departments. In seeking ways of overcoming the problem and preventing further increases, health-education campaigns have been organized at Federal and 'Land' levels. The Federal government has established a Central Health-Education Unit which works together with representatives from each of the states within the federation. The unit produces and tests materials which can be used by nurses, teachers and other community workers.

Most impressive is the teaching package, which has an academic and research basis, and consists of a loose-leaf tome of over 500 pages. The book is divided into sections which detail the size and nature of the problem, related problems, legal aspects, objectives for teaching and learning, lesson plans and preparations. The latter could be used for lecturing without alteration, or the material can be used in sections as discussion topics. The book also gives suggestions for approaches to different age groups, for use in varying settings and in different lengths of time. It also suggests projects and tasks for students to complete. Additionally the package contains transparencies, acetates and other teaching aids (Noack et al., 1980). The central agency also publishes a magazine, freely available, looking something like a horror 'Beano' to attract and inform the general public, especially adolescents.

The combined national and local effort is very substantial, but it has not yet been demonstrated that it will achieve its aims, or how much adaptation and addition is required by field workers in order to make the material relevant to their particular needs and situations. Having carefully scrutinized the teaching package and other materials, the suspicion is that it is like the proverbial 'curate's egg' — good in parts — but that it requires professional skills, time and effort to make it an adequate tool for the trade of health education.

It has already been stated that in Germany, and Europe generally, including the United Kingdom, any health-education action vies with commercial interests. However, the German government have taken account of this, and in 1979 passed legislation which now requires every insurance company that wishes to be part of the national insurance facility to channel 10% of its profits into preventive measures. The law became operational in 1981 and, therefore, the results are yet to come, but it should provide substantially increased resources for health education and other preventive efforts. Germany has no National Health Service like Britain, but each employee and employer are required to subscribe to an insurance scheme. Approximately 1400 companies are approved by the Federal government to provide coverage for health and sickness services. The companies base their payments to professional practitioners and institutions on a system of 'items-of-service', neither prevention nor health education are easily accountable in those terms.

America

The biggest and wealthiest developed country is usually considered to be the United States of America. Despite, or because of, its apparent wealth, there are as many or more, and very similar, health problems being described as anywhere else in the world. To date there is no nationwide programme or policy on prevention and health education. Many states show evidence of activity in these fields, and there has been relevant legislation in a few states. The scope of activities, who the practitioners are, what qualifications and skills they possess depends on the policies and politics of each state. Training programmes for health professionals, as one aspect of their progression to graduate status, include preparation for the practice of health education. This element is very strong in the masters programmes of nurse practitioners.

One of the biggest problems facing health educators, and somewhat at variance from those facing their European colleagues, is that, in general, United States citizens regard state intervention as a threat to their independence, or an invasion of their privacy. They are likely to resent any professional approach not invited or initiated by themselves. Health education is, therefore, perceived as provision for the poor, needy or inept — despite health statistics which prove the contrary. The challenge this poses to health educators is, therefore, increased, they have to add diplomacy and extra perseverance to their range of skills. Included in the report of the 10th international conference, already quoted, is a very clear description of one way Americans are striving and winning towards achievements in health education. In very large measure the difficulties of practice in America are being overcome through the enthusiasm and professionalism of health educators, most of whom are trained nurses. Many American nurses visit Britain and other European countries to study the methods used, and on their return are making great inroads into establishing effective practice.

Further afield

Developing countries are evolving many different, imaginative programmes of health education. The most common practice is to provide local, untrained assistants with sufficient and accurate information, and agree a programme with them in which they use their new found knowledge to pass onto the inhabitants of their village or district. By this means any health message is relevant to the current situation, acceptable in terms of the person providing the teaching, and usually put in a manner and idiom which is understandable to the people for whom the message is designed. In turn the untrained health worker can, and does, communicate the most urgent health needs to policy makers and planners. Many untrained health educators become very expert at their tasks, a proportion showing such capabilities that they go on to receive training and participate in health teaching on a broader front, as well as becoming more and more involved with planning and provision of health care which will be appropriate for their community.

It is often said that health education in developing countries is difficult because of the superstitions or religious practices of the population, in fact, where local workers and teachers share the beliefs of his or her clientele this poses less of a problem than some of the firmly held convictions of the populations and the mixture of attitudes held by groups within developed countries.

Incentive schemes have been tried, such as the much reported free gifts of transistor radios in India for those who practice family limitation. Such schemes have proved to be of limited value; the reward of achieving improvements, which can be maintained fairly long term, in family health and especially the health of children and the means of sustaining an active life, are generally accepted to be sufficient of themselves.

One example of success is splendidly presented in a film made by the Commonwealth Society for the Blind. The film shows the medical treatment given, at minimal cost, to those thousands of people suffering from eye diseases and the efforts taking place alongside to improve standards of sanitation and hygiene to prevent recurrence of disease and decreased incidence. Doctors and nurses cope with hundreds of patients and their relatives and companions, who may be composed of the whole village, at one session, other nurses and volunteers demonstrate to them how to utilize their resources, especially the scarce water supplies. Instruction on how to prepare foods, and demonstrations on how nutrition can be improved even in the poorest circumstances form part of the teaching. The audience find health teaching a strange phenomenon, but are willing to listen and are prepared to try the suggestions as they are as keen as the health workers to improve their existence. Better nutrition, if it means less eye trouble, can lead to being able to function, earn and therefore maintain and improve the standard of living, it does not require formal schooling to understand these facts but the stimuli provided by health educators is sufficient.

The World Health Organization

The World Health Organization acts as a catalyst in the efforts made throughout its member countries. It fully supports, through funds and trained experts, a multitude of schemes, finances research into health problems, publishes journals and booklets in many languages on general topics and specific subjects, and assists in the training of local workers and professionals. It also plays a co-ordinating role in channelling international resources to be used to maximum possible effect.

In 1981, as part of the on-going dialogue among health workers, especially those providing primary health care in Europe, WHO supported a conference on the role of the health visitor/public-health nurse. This conference was attended by 140 people from 15 countries, and the lovely setting of Danbury, Essex provided the background for much fruitful and heated debate. One theme which recurred was the need for improved teaching during the prenatal period and to parents with young children. The other recurrent theme was how nurses could influence policies and politicians to obtain improved facilities, staff and resources. It is hoped that this conference will prove to be one of a series for those working at field level, and that it will assist in promoting international understanding and a concerted move towards the aim of 'health for all by the year 2000' the stated objective of WHO and Alma-Ata (Wilson, 1982).

General efforts

Several other means of giving health messages internationally have been tried, and new means are suggested periodically. Some of these are considered to be successful, but no overall evaluation has been carried out so far. It may be impossible to perform a valid evaluation as one of the unknown factors is the extent to which the message has been received or understood. In some cases it would be difficult to identify the recipients of the message. Some of the means are random and hope to reach a varied and multiple audience by going through several processes and by selecing a target which has to pass through other possible intermediate targets.

Postal services

One relatively common way of sending a health-education message is through the postal services, by using the cancellation on the envelope to express the goal. Antismoking notices have appeared on letters and parcels, as have exhortations to use safety precautions at work and play. It would be of great interest whether this is noticed by recipients and other handlers of postal materials, or whether it is of interest to collectors only.

Postage stamps are a colourful means of alerting people to dangers to health. Philatelic exhibitions contain many frames of stamps depicting various routes to health, and the presentation packs give greater details to mainly young recipients. One German series of stamps detailed every possible hazard found in factories and other work places, as well as such commons hazards as faulty electric plugs. The series was in use for more than a year — did it achieve a reduction in accidents? No evidence is available to answer that question. Many countries throughout the world have used this means of health education, it is attractive and costs no more than the normal cost involved in issuing stamps. The size of the stamp has, however, not been varied to see whether this might have a greater or lesser effect. The rationale leading to these efforts, apart from the cost factor, is that they are not selective of any group or target, and thereby not offensive to anyone, and that they are likely to reach more people than any other method, including those who do not listen to instructive programmes on radio or television, read books or journals, look at posters, attend cinemas or are in receipt of professional services or care. One estimate suggests that the categories listed form 80% of the total populations, and that only the remaining 20% are in contact with possible health educators.

International theme-related years

Each year is, nowadays, given a theme of international relevance. Of special interest to those involved in health education have been the International Year of the Disabled Person (IYDP) in 1981 and the International Year of the Child in 1980. During these years there were many events, internationally, nationally and locally, to stimulate interest in the stated category, and to increase awareness and knowledge about all aspects relating to the chosen field, as well as highlighting the problems surrounding the group. The nature of any related activity depends on the organizers of the events. The secondary objective, though one could be forgiven for thinking that it was the primary one, is to stimulate action on behalf of the particular group, at all levels ranging from changes in legislation to support for individuals and their families.

The stated aims of subject- or category-biased international years appear commendable, but there is a dangerous dichotomy between the ideal and its effects. 1981 proved itself a difficult year for many handicapped or disabled persons. Not only was awareness of their needs created among the general public of most countries, but disabled people became much more aware of the life and facilities which might be feasible for them, and which could be considered desirable or even their basic human right. In many instances it was impossible to obtain the resources, be they money, equipment or manpower, to meet the demand thus created. Hopefully the efforts of IYDP were not wasted, but it will take a long time, possibly a decade, to reach the desired goals. In the meantime there is the danger that the impetus and pressure may be lost, and long-term achievements fall below the proven potential. Also, in the meantime, health-care workers and social workers are having to cope with the problems of dissatisfied and unhappy clients and their families. The extent of disenchantment and disappointment created among disabled people is immeasurable and may prove to have serious consequences.

The way forward

The most immediate way forward for those professionals whose role and function includes health education, is to learn from each other and to help each other as much as possible. International exchange visits and joint projects are becoming acceptable practice, though still difficult to accomplish and arrange. Many sources (Wilson, 1982) urge that such exchanges should become a regular feature of professional practice in future, no amount of written texts or film can replace the value of personal contact.

The implementation of the EEC directives for nursing education and training will ensure that each trained nurse in the member countries has the foundation during his or her training to become a health educator, the revised form of training will also make mobility between countries a reality. This should be the start and stimulus to go forward together towards shared information, planning of health-care programmes — inclusive of health education — and shared evaluation and research. It remains a challenging prospect — but challenges are the precursors of success.

Further reading

De Bono, E (1982) Thinking Course, BBC publications

Europe — News/Novelles/Neuigkeiten/HOBOCTN (bi-monthly), Mrs R Erben, Director of the IUHE European Bureau, c/o BZgA, 200 Osterheimer Strasse, 5 Koln-Merheim, Germany

HEC (1980) Health education in action; achievement and priorities, Report of the 10th International Conference on Health Education, Health Education Council, London and Scottish Health Education Group, Edinburgh

Kaplun, A and Erben, R (1980) Health Education in Europe, International Journal of Health Education, Geneva

Noack, K A et al. (1980) Gesundheitserziehung und Schule—Illegale Drogen, Arzneimittelmisbrauch, Alkohol, Rauchen, Bundeszentrale fur Gesundheitliche Aufklaring, Koln, Ernst Klett, Stuttgart

Wilson, C T editor (1982) Primary Health Care in Europe — The Role of the Health Visitor, NELP, London

APPENDIX I

DEFINITIONS OF HEALTH AND HEALTH EDUCATION

Health, which is a state of complete physical, mental and social well-being and not merely the absence of disease or infirmity, is a *fundamental human right*.

WHO (1978) Declaration of the Conference on Primary Health Care,
Alma-Ata, 1978

Health designates a process of adaptation, the ability to accept changing environments, to growing up, to ageing, to healing when damaged, to suffering and to the peaceful expectation of death.

I Illich (1977) Disabling Professions, Marion Boyars

Health is a precarious state, which augurs no good. Health is a potentiality, the ability of the individual or social group to be in continuous change, in order not only to function better in the present, but also to prepare for the future.

R Dubos, Biologist

Health is a purchasable commodity of which a community can possess, within limits, as much or as little as it cares to pay for.

R H Tawney (1931) Equality, Allen & Unwin

Health is a condition that maximizes the individual's capacity to live happily and productively, that is the degree to which he is able to carry on his usual activities, or the level he can achieve, within the limits of pre-existing disease, disability or genetic endowment.

R Murray and J Zeater (1970) Nursing Concepts for Health Promotion,
Prentice Hall

Health is a purposeful, adaptive response, physically, mentally and socially, to internal and external stimuli, in order to maintain stability and comfort.

R Murray and J Zeater (1970) Nursing Concepts for Health Promotion, Prentice Hall

Health is that state of moral, mental and physical well-being which enables a man to face any crisis in life with the utmost facility and grace.

Pericles, c A.D. 400

Health education is the provision and reinforcement of information to enable individuals to assess risks to health and to use the health and social services when appropriate.

C Farrel and R Levitt (1980) Consumers, Community health councils and the NHS, KF Project Paper RC8, King's Fund Centre

It is difficult to fix precise boundaries to health education. We have regarded health education as being involved where the prime purpose of information or instruction is to promote mental or physical health.

Lord Cohen of Birkenhead (1964) — Inquiry into Health Education, DHSS Cohen Report

... the focus of health education is on people and on action. In general its aims are to persuade people to adopt and sustain healthful life practices, to use judiciously and wisely the health services available to them and to take their own decisions, both individually and collectively to improve their health status and environment.

WHO Expert Committee on Health Education, 1969

Health education concerns all those experiences of an individual, group or community that influence beliefs, attitudes and behaviour with respect to health as well as the processes and efforts of producing change when this is necessary for optimal health.

WHO, Research in Health Education, 1969

Objectives of NHS for health education "to contribute to the improvement of the quality of life of the individual and the enhancement of his capacity to use his abilities to the greatest possible extent".

K Richards (1980) The NHS and Social Services, KF Project Paper RC11,
King's Fund Centre

Health education = reduction of ignorance. It should be a form of advertising and like advertisers should be aware of the variety of responses, leading to free, that is, informed consumer choice.

David Cohen (1981) Prevention as an Economic Good,
Aberdeen University

Prevention is analogous to saving and therefore not attractive when income or immediate return is seen to be low. Health education is not prevention, only its tool.

Health education is the rehumanization of professional health care ...

D Marsden Wagner (1978) Introduction to Policy on Primary Health Care
WHO

Instead of blaming, health promotion should be a process of empowering people to take control over, and responsibility for, their health.

S Penfold, University of British Columbia (victim blaming,
the perfect cop-out)

In the widest sense, health education may be defined as the sum total of all influences that collectively determine knowledge, belief, a behaviour related to the promotion, maintenance and restoration of health in individuals and communities.

Professor Alwyn Smith (1978) Address to faculty University of Manchester

Health education includes the aspect of motivation which assists the person to take the information and do something with it to keep himself healthier.

US Department of Health Education Welfare (1973) Policy Document on
Health Education

APPENDIX II

DECLARATION OF ALMA–ATA

The International Conference on Primary Health Care, meeting in Alma-Ata this 12th day of September in the year 1978, expressing the need for urgent action by all governments, all health and development workers, and the world community to protect and promote the health of all the people of the world, hereby makes the folowing declaration:

1. The conference strongly reaffirms that health, which is a state of complete physical, mental and social well-being, and not merely the absence of disease or infirmity, is a fundamental human right and that the attainment of the highest possible level of health is a most important world-wide social goal whose realization requires the action of many other social and economic sectors in addition to the health sector.

2. The existing gross inequality in the health status of the people, particularly between developed and developing countries as well as within countries, is politically, socially and economically unacceptable and is, therefore, of common concern to all countries.

3. Economic and social development, based on a new international economic order, is of basic importance to the fullest attainment of health for all and to the reduction of the gap between the health status of the developing and developed countries. The promotion and protection of the health of the people is essential to sustained economic and social development and contributes to a better quality of life and to world peace.

4. The people have the right and duty to participate individually and collectively in the planning and implementation of their health care.

5. Governments have a responsibility for the health of their people which can be fulfilled only by the provision of adequate health and social measures. A main social target of governments, international organizations, and the whole world community in the coming

decades should be the attainment by all peoples of the world by the year 2000 of a level of health that will permit them to lead a socially and economically productive life. Primary health care is the key to attaining this target as part of development in the spirit of social justice.

6. Primary health care is essential health care based on practical scientifically sound and socially acceptable methods and technology made universally accessible to individuals and families in the community through their full participation and at a cost that the community and country can afford to maintain at every stage of their development in the spirit of self-reliance and self-determination. It forms an integral part both of the country's health system, of which it is the central function and main focus, and of the overall social and economic development of the community. It is the first level of contact of individuals, the family and community with the national health system, bringing health care as close as possible to where people live and work, and constitutes the first element of a continuing health-care process.

7. Primary health care:
   (i) reflects and evolves from the economic conditions and sociocultural and political characteristics of the country and its communities and is based on the application of the relevant results of social, biomedical and health services research and public health experience;
   (ii) addresses the main health problems in the community, providing promotive, preventive, curative and rehabilitative services accordingly;
   (iii) includes at least: education concerning prevailing health problems and the methods of preventing and controlling them; promotion of food supply and proper nutrition; an adequate supply of safe water and basic sanitation; maternal and child health care, including family planning; immunization against the major infectious diseases; prevention and control of locally endemic diseases; appropriate treatment of common diseases and injuries; and provision of essential drugs;
   (iv) involves, in addition to the health sector, all related sectors and aspects of national and community development, in particular agriculture, animal husbandry, food, industry, education,

housing, public works, communications, and other sectors; and demands the co-ordinated efforts of all those sectors;

(v) requires and promotes maximum community and individual self-reliance and participation in the planning, organization, operation and control of primary health care, making fullest use of local, national and other available resources; and to this end develops through appropriate education the ability of communities to participate;

(vi) should be sustained by integrated, functional and mutually supportive referral systems, leading to the progressive improvement of comprehensive health care for all, and giving priority to those most in need;

(vii) relies, at local and referral levels, on health workers, including physicians, nurses, midwives, auxiliaries and community workers as applicable, as well as traditional practitioners as needed, suitably trained socially and technically to work as a health team and to respond to the expressed health needs of the community.

8. All governments should formulate national policies, strategies and plans of action to launch and sustain primary health care as part of a comprehensive national health system and in co-ordination with other sectors. To this end it will be necessary to exercise political will, to mobilize the country's resources and to use available external resources rationally.

9. All countries should co-operate in a spirit of partnership and service to ensure primary health care for all people, since the attainment of health by people in any one country directly concerns and benefits every other country. In this context the joint WHO/UNICEF report on primary health care constitutes a solid basis for the further development and operation of primary health care throughout the world.

10. An acceptable level of health for all the people of the world by the year 2000 can be attained through a fuller and better use of the world's resources, a considerable part of which is now spent on armaments and military conflicts. A genuine policy of independence, peace, detente and disarmament could and should release additional resources that could well be devoted to peaceful aims and in particular to the acceleration of social and economic development of

which primary health care, as an essential part, should be allotted its proper share.

The International Conference on Primary Health Care calls for urgent and effective national and international action to develop and implement primary health care through the world and particularly in developing countries in a spirit of technical co-operation and in keeping with a new international economic order. It urges governments, WHO, UNICEF and other international organizations, as well as multilateral and bilateral agencies, nongovernmental organizations, funding agencies, all health workers and the whole world community to support national and international commitment to primary health care and to channel increased technical and financial support to it, particularly in developing countries. The conference calls on all the aforementioned to collaborate in introducing, developing and maintaining primary health care in accordance with the spirit and content of this declaration.

WHO (1978) Report on the Primary Health Care Conference,
Alma Ata, 1978, Reprinted with permission.

INDEX

181